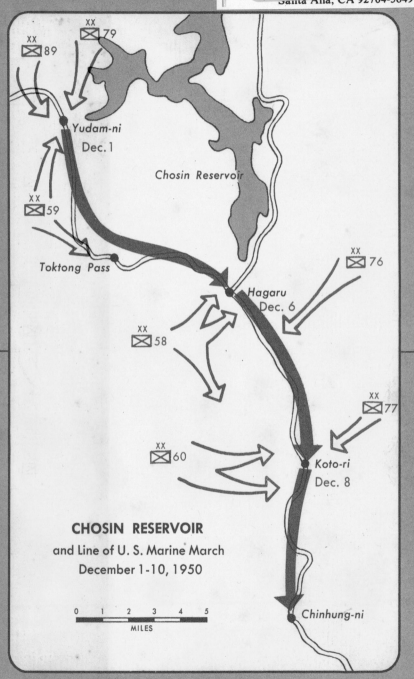

XX
89

XX
79

Yudam-ni
Dec. 1

Chosin Reservoir

XX
59

Toktong Pass

XX
76

Hagaru
Dec. 6

XX
58

XX
77

XX
60

Koto-ri
Dec. 8

CHOSIN RESERVOIR
and Line of U. S. Marine March
December 1-10, 1950

0   1   2   3   4   5
MILES

Chinhung-ni

THE MARCH TO GLORY

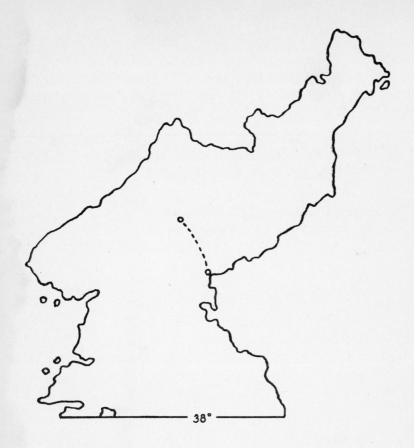

38°

THE MARCH TO GLORY

ROBERT LECKIE

THE WORLD PUBLISHING COMPANY
CLEVELAND AND NEW YORK

Published by THE WORLD PUBLISHING COMPANY
2231 West 110th Street, Cleveland 2, Ohio

Published simultaneously in Canada by
NELSON, FOSTER & SCOTT LTD.

Library of Congress Catalog Card Number: 60-11454

First Edition

To Those Who Marched, To Those Who Led —
To Those Who Dare To Follow

ACKNOWLEDGMENTS

The material used in writing this book has come
come from two sources. The first and most important was
the personal recollections of those scores of survivors of
the Chosin Reservoir campaign who were kind enough to
grant the author interviews or to correspond with him. The
second was a mass of published or classified material, the
study of which occupied the author for about a year before
the business of interviewing could be begun. This included
histories of Korea, military histories of the Korean fighting,
Special Action Reports, official unit histories, battalion
diaries, and combat interviews, as well as maps, photographs,
and other classified documents to which the Department of
the Navy generously—though carefully—granted the author
clearance and access. Professional monographs, citations,
newspaper articles, and magazine pieces also were used. Because this book does not pretend to be a technical work, but
rather the story of an ordeal sustained by flesh-and-blood
Americans, it does not seem necessary to attach a biblio-
graphy to it. Should some indication of the extent of the
author's research be required, suffice it to say that the classified material alone filled a four-drawer filing cabinet at the
Marine Historical Branch in Washington. Those who may be
inclined to go beyond this unofficial account may consult the
excellent, complete, and official *U.S. Marine Operations in
Korea*, Vol. 3, by Lynn Montross and Captain Nicholas A.

8 ACKNOWLEDGMENTS

Canzona, which may be obtained from the Government Printing Office.

Nevertheless, a word of thanks is due to those who assisted the author along his way. First, let me thank the U.S. Secretary of Defense, the Department of the Navy, and the U.S. Marine Corps, especially its commandant, General David M. Shoup. My gratitude also goes out to Brigadier General Avery R. Kier, who was the Director, Division of Information, U.S.M.C., at the time I began my research, and to Colonel Donald R. Nugent, his successor. My most able pilot through official channels has been Lieutenant Colonel Philip N. Pierce of that Division's Media Branch, and my guide through a maze of classified material was Mr. Daniel M. O'Quinlivan, Head, Research & Records, Marine Historical Branch. Also, my thanks are due to Mrs. Martha Holler of the Defense Department's Accreditation and Travel Division; Colonel William M. Miller, Commanding Officer, Marine Historical Branch; Mr. Lynn Montross, the well-known Marine historian and military critic; Colonel John Stage of the Marine Corps Air Station, El Toro, California; Lieutenant General E. W. Snedeker, Commanding General of the Marine Base at Quantico, Virginia; Major General Francis M. McAllister, Commanding General, Department of the Pacific; Colonel Donald L. Dickson, editor, *The Leatherneck Magazine;* and Lieutenant Colonel Thomas N. Greene, editor, *Marine Corps Gazette.* In one way or another, with criticism, with suggestions, by furnishing transportation or material, these persons have been of assistance to the author.

I wish also to acknowledge a special debt to the noted military historian and analyst, Brigadier General S. L. A. Marshall, U.S.A.R. I am indebted to General Marshall not only for his helpful suggestions on the writing of this book, but also for his great generosity in allowing me to use numerous combat interviews obtained by him immediately after the Marines came down The Road to the sea.

Of all the Chosin Reservoir participants I have interviewed, none was more gracious and helpful than the man who commanded that epic feat of arms—General Oliver P. Smith, U.S.M.C. (Ret.). In the course of a six-hour interview, General Smith exhausted an interrogator many years his junior. And I am similarly grateful to Lieutenant General Lewis B. Puller, U.S.M.C. (Ret.), and Lieutenant General Homer L. Litzenberg, U.S.M.C. (Ret.). These two general officers and Brigadier General Raymond L. Murray, U.S.M.C., with whom I corresponded to my decided advantage, were commanders of the First Division's infantry regiments at Chosin. Though I corresponded with General Murray, my plans to visit him on Okinawa—where he is Assistant Division Commander, Third Marine Division—were wrecked by a combination of weather delays and deadlines.

Among those junior officers and former enlisted men to whom I am particularly indebted are Major William Barber and Messrs. Robert Kennemore and Hector Cafferata, three Medal of Honor winners whose individual stories reflect the magnificent *esprit* which brought the Marines through in Korea. In addition to these, there were many other Marines and former Marines who consented to questioning by the author or who corresponded with him. To all of them, my deepest thanks and appreciation—and if there is not the space here to thank each one separately, then it is hoped that this book will serve as their reward, as it may also stand for their splendid comrades who marched and fought along that dreadful Road.

R.L.

With one exception, all names used herein are true. All ranks are those held at the time. All mileages, estimates of Chinese strength, estimates of Chinese casualties, figures for our own strength and casualties, are from official records of the United States Marine Corps. Though the use of military jargon has been avoided almost completely here, there are a few words and phrases that may need to be defined. These are:

BAR   Browning Automatic Rifle, or light machine gun, weighing 19.4 pounds complete with its bipod and 20-round magazine.

CP   Command Post, or the field headquarters of any commander from a platoon leader (lieutenant) up to a regiment (colonel).

HOWITZER   A short-barreled artillery piece. Its high trajectory, as opposed to the flat arc of the long-barreled artillery rifle, makes it suitable for mountain warfare.

M-1   The Garand semiautomatic rifle which fires a
             clip of eight rounds of .30 caliber ammunition
             —standard weapon of the U.S. infantryman
             in 1950.

MORTAR   A smooth-bored steel tube which is fired by
             dropping shells down its muzzle. Its high-angle
             fire makes it an ideal front-line weapon. It is
             easily disassembled and can be carried by a few
             men.

Finally, the basic force in this campaign was the infantry
or rifle battalion, which, with its attached troops, is a unit
of between 1,000 and 1,500 men. The battalion is usually
composed of three line companies and a headquarters company. These companies have alphabetical names: A, B, and
C for a first battalion; D, E, and F for a second battalion;
G, H, and I for a third battalion. To avoid a confusing
sameness of sound during battle, these alphabetical desig-
nations are given names: Able for A, Baker for B, Charlie
for C, Dog for D, Easy for E, Fox for F, George for G,
How for H, and Item for I. A company has four platoons
composed of four squads of about ten men each. With its
own special troops, a company has a strength of between
200 and 250 men.

There are three battalions to a regiment, and a regiment
can reach a strength of between 3,000 and 4,500 men. There
are three line regiments and an artillery regiment to a division. The line regiments of the First Marine Division are
the First, Fifth, and Seventh, and the artillery regiment is
the Eleventh. At full strength a Marine division can carry
25,000 men on its roster, because, being a self-sufficient am-
phibious force, it requires an enormous number of supporting
troops. In effect, a Marine division is a small army.

DISTANCES BETWEEN TOWNS

Hungnam to Hamhung	8 miles
Hamhung to Sudong	29
Sudong to Chinhung-ni	6
Chinhung-ni to Koto-ri	10
Koto-ri to Hagaru-ri	11
Hagaru-ri to Yudam-ni	14
Total Distance	78 miles

THE MARCH TO GLORY

CHAPTER ONE

THE Road runs seventy-eight miles from the port
of Hungnam on the east coast of North Korea to the tiny
village of Yudam-ni, caught in a cup of steep bare hills to
the west of Chosin Reservoir. It runs north, turning and
twisting west while making the ascent from the railhead
at Chinhung-ni to gain the four-thousand-foot plateau
supporting the towns of Koto-ri and Hagaru-ri, before
plunging and winding down to Yudam-ni.

It is a narrow road, nameless as the cold Korean hills
it traverses, unpaved, rocky—in summer a mire, in winter
a frozen spiral off which bullets will spang with the sound
of lead striking steel. It is wide enough to permit the
passage of a single truck. Where it curls about the ridge
shelves, it can be widened to allow the cautious progress
of a tank.

It runs through level valleys and crosses watercourses.
Rising to the hills, it hugs the slopes—shying away from
gorges and abysses that fall away to left or right.

It is a road made for ambush, and in that cold November of 1950 it led America's First Marine Division into a
trap.

CHAPTER TWO

In that November of 1950 the Korean War was not yet half a year old. It had been barely five months since the North Korean Reds had launched their furious charge down the peninsula, sweeping the crumbling South Korean armies before them, capturing Seoul, threatening to "unify" the divided nation beneath the sign of the hammer and sickle before the stunned West could intervene.

Once again this little land—this Hermit Kingdom with a tradition of isolation and a history of foreign invasion —was in flames. But she no longer burned on the altar of Chinese or Japanese or Czarist Russian territorial ambition. Now she flamed in a civil war—Korean against Korean under the rival banners of the two great contending ideologies which had sundered the world into hostile camps. This was the misfortune which befell this poor and mountainous country not five years after the Japanese occupation had ended with Nippon's unconditional surrender.

It had been American military might that had brought imperial Japan to her knees. Our Western Allies had helped very little. Communist Russia had done nothing.

Moreover Stalin did not declare war on Japan until August 8, 1945—two days after the world's first atomic bomb fell on Hiroshima. Though Russia had waited almost four years to decide that Japan was her enemy, she issued her declaration of war with great speed.

After Hiroshima Japan began sinking fast. In a few days the war would be over. Russia could not afford to wait longer, she had to be in on the kill if she wanted to make her customary demand for the lion's share of the flesh. On August 8, she declared war. On August 12—four days before Japan capitulated—the vanguard of a quarter million Communist troops entered northern Korea.

They entered under the terms of concessions made to Stalin at Yalta by President Roosevelt, and they entered after having overrun Manchuria, stripping it of all industrial booty, accepting the surrender of 600,000 Japanese soldiers and spiriting most of these off to Siberia as slaves. All this was gained at the expense of a few token shots fired between August 8 and August 12, and then the Communists began speedily dismantling and carrying off from 30 to 40 per cent of the industrial plant of northern Korea. Thus engaged, the Soviets paid little attention to the southern half of the Korean peninsula, that part which had fallen to United States trusteeship. For South Korea was the poorer half of a poor land. It was agricultural. It had most of the people—20,000,000 as opposed to the 8,000,000 in North Korea—but very little of the wealth. Most of Korea's industry was concentrated in the north.

In the years between the end of World War II and the outbreak of war in Korea, the Russians carefully cultivated a Communist puppet government. They welshed on terms of the Moscow Conference of 1945 guaranteeing democratic elections for the whole nation, once the trusteeship phase had ended. They sabotaged the attempts of the Soviet-American Joint Commission to bring this about. Finally in 1948, at the request of the United States, the United Nations resolved that all the people of Korea be given a chance to elect a national assembly. A commission was formed to supervise the voting. The Reds barred its members from entering North Korea. Elections were only held in the south, where in May a government under President Syngman Rhee was elected, with a capital at Seoul. The Communists retaliated by electing their own government in the north, with a capital in Pyongyang. The United States and the UN refused to recognize it, and the Reds replied by snubbing the government to the south.

Now the stage was set. Though brothers of one blood, the Koreans of the north and south faced each other across the 38th Parallel, exchanging insults and taunts—and in the case of the Communists, pursuing the vendetta to the extent of shutting off the power which flowed south from northern hydroelectric plants. They were divided by different ideologies, and only different religions can cause brother to hate brother more. While the United States, fearing censure as a warmonger, carefully refrained from developing South Korean military strength beyond the police-force stage, the Communists in the north began building the North Korean People's Army. Even when the Russians, with great fanfare, withdrew their military at the end of 1948, they left expert string-pullers behind them to manipulate the puppet government and army they had created.

A year later China fell to the Communists. By the end of 1949 the Nationalist forces of Generalissimo Chiang Kai-shek had been beaten. All China went to the Reds, including Manchuria which borders Korea at the Yalu

River. With the end of the fighting, thousands upon thousands of Koreans who had fought for Communist China came swarming over the border to join the North Korean People's Army. And the Red government of North Korea was now backed by a powerful ally across the Yalu.

By the following spring war might have been foreseen as inevitable, for the Communists in North Korea were already talking peace. Even as Radio Pyongyang spoke soulfully of peaceful unification of all Korea, General Nam Il was bringing his striking force of nine infantry divisions and one armored division down to the 38th Parallel.

On June 25, 1950, they charged south.

The world seemed to teeter on the brink of a third world war in those fateful closing days of June, while President Truman, acting swiftly, sent American troops by air to Korea from Japan. Then, on a lucky day on which the Soviet Union had decided to boycott the United Nations Security Council, a UN "police force" was voted and placed under the command of General of the Army Douglas MacArthur. It was, in the main, American. United States soldiers rallied the routed South Koreans behind a perimeter, or defensive arc, thrown up at the port of Pusan on the peninsula's southeastern tip. There forces were built up, among them the First Marine Provisional Brigade, which was later to be expanded into that First Marine Division of World War II glory. The soldiers and Marines stopped the Red rush. The line steadied. The North Korean "unification drive" was blunted.

Then followed the master stroke. Never again would the military genius of Douglas MacArthur shine as brilliantly as in the following September. Up around the west coast of South Korea sailed the Tenth Corps, spearheaded

by the First Marine Division. Thrusting up from Pusan
came the UN's Eighth Army. The Marines stormed ashore
at Inchon, scaling those steep tidal mudbanks and driving
across the Han River in a ten-day running battle that
ended with the recapture of Seoul.

The Tenth Corps and the Eighth Army soon began to
grind the North Koreans to bits. In less than two months
total victory for the Communists was being turned into
something akin to total defeat. Beaten, the Reds wheeled
and fled. They recrossed the 38th Parallel. They streamed
homeward, their commanders hoping that distance, the
premature onslaught of that incredibly severe Korean
winter, or, perhaps even then, direct intervention by their
Communist Chinese allies across the Yalu River might
save them from annihilation.

MacArthur pursued. His forces crossed the 38th Parallel and entered North Korea. In this thrust the Eighth
Army struck on the left and the Tenth Corps on the right.
Again the decks of transport ships rolled and pitched beneath the "boondockers" of the men of the First Marine
Division. They were sailing around the peninsula and up
the east, or right, side of North Korea. They came ashore
at Wonsan, unopposed—in fact, embarrassed, for the
comedian Bob Hope and his singing girls were there to
greet them. It was great fun for the soldiers and sailors
who witnessed their chagrin, but very poor comedy to
Marines.

Korea began to look like a phony war to them. True,
there was more fighting with the Reds. Here a train might
be ambushed by one of many bands of guerrillas who had
taken to the hills, there a pitched battle might be fought.
Yet the fighting had a desultory nature. It possessed all
the marks of a mopping-up operation. The plight of the

North Koreans was known. They were disorganized, often without officers. They were cold. Many had thrown away their weapons. By day they hid in the villages—by night they foraged for food. A spirit of confidence, a false sense of easy victory, began to take hold of the men of the First Marine Division.

"Hell, man, you know I ain't seen a gook face to face since we landed at Inchon? Every time I bayonet one, I stick him in the back. You ask me, this war's just about over!"

So it seemed, and as October turned into November, confidence turned into cockiness.

"You hear the scuttlebutt? We're goin' home for Christmas!"

"Aw, blow it. Who says so?"

"Dugout Doug."

"MacArthur! Now, if that ain't a crock o' crap, I never—"

"All right, you stay here, then. Me, I'm writing the old lady to lay out the dress blues and stand by!"

That was the talk in the foxhole outposts or in the squad tents. Even an issue of cold-weather clothing did little to puncture that ballooning "Home-for-Christmas" spirit.

And then the First Marine Division took The Road.

They set their faces northward toward Koto-ri and Hagaru-ri and Yudam-ni and the light blue sheet of ice that was Chosin Reservoir. They were part of the right-hand column of the general assault to the Yalu with which General MacArthur proposed to end the war.

And coming down to meet them, to gird them in a ring of steel and ice and hostile flesh, were two new enemies: the Korean cold and the Communist Chinese.

CHAPTER THREE

WINTER in North Korea is a cold white howling beast. Nothing moves but the bitter wind, rising off the Manchurian plain, sweeping over the desolated mountain peaks, whistling down the valleys. It freezes rivers, chokes the gorges with snow and glazes the rocks with ice. By day the temperature rises, hovering somewhere between zero and 20 degrees. With dark, coming about five o'clock, it falls rapidly. By four in the morning, it may stand at 20 degrees below zero, perhaps as much as 30 degrees below.

It is not a dry cold. It is a wet, raw, devouring cold. The Marines had never known such cold before, much less lived out in it or fought in it. Even the veterans of Iceland or those old "China hands" with the deep windburn and the hard lips could find no breath to boast in it. In such cold, weapons freeze, rations freeze, human flesh freezes. The carbine becomes a useless stick. It will not fire, for the gases generated by burning powder are too weak to move its parts. It has no worth as a club, for its slender stock is frozen brittle and it will break. Rifle barrels become corroded and pitted from being fired, and though the M-1 rifle will resist the cold, its moving parts must not be oiled too heavily, or they will freeze solid.

Nor will artillery pieces fire rapidly. The 105mm howitzer, once fired, will not leap back instantly into position. It will creep back—in thirty seconds or more. Ammunition freezes, too. Shells do not go off, and if they have been air-dropped, perhaps only 25 per cent will survive the impact of collision with that rocklike earth. Grenades do not explode, and flares fizzle into impotence within the freezing dark. The jackets of water-cooled machine guns, the "heavies," as they are called, must be filled with antifreeze. If it is not available, they must be fired once in every two hours or so, like the air-cooled "lights." If not, they freeze. Mortars, those faithful "stovepipes" that kill men, will work reasonably well—but the square base plates to which they are fastened are liable to break in two when the recoil slams them against the frozen ground. Then, in battle, Marines will hold them in their hands, risking burns and blisters on their frozen fingers.

Few foxholes are dug in the North Korean cold. Frost level sinks to a depth of fourteen inches. Entrenching tools break in two within a very few strokes. Sometimes, if explosive is available, holes will be dynamited for the machine guns. Or riflemen will squeeze their chilled bodies into rocky crevices or gain cover behind naked boulders. In extremity after a battle a position may be barricaded with the frozen bodies of the enemy.

In such cold, mechanization breaks down. A tanker or a trucker may need as much as two hours to refuel his vehicle. Hands made bulky by mittens with inserts for the trigger fingers fumble at a task normally requiring minutes. And no man thoughtlessly removes those gloves for long. Frostbite will stiffen his fingers, and he may lose

them. Nor will any man lay a naked hand against his
weapon barrel or the steel hide of a tank. If he does, and
pulls the hand away, five bloody marks will bear testimony
to his carelessness. And tankers and truckers must cherish
their batteries with the care an infantryman accords his
rifle. If engines are not run for a quarter-hour in every
two, the batteries will not work again.

A man living and fighting in such cold will wear his
clothing in layers. He will have heavy underwear and a
sweater and trousers and over this a field jacket and over
all a parka. He will find it difficult to see to right or left,
marching and fighting like a horse with blinders. His feet
will be covered with layers of woolen socks—two pairs,
perhaps three—and these will be stuffed into buckskin
boots or perhaps those shoe-pacs of recent issue. But the
shoe-pacs become a refrigerator for the unwary. They
are rubberized. As a man moves in them, his feet sweat.
When he stands still, the sweat freezes into a film of ice
lying between his foot and the inner sole. If he does not
remove his shoe-pacs from time to time to rub his feet, he
will fall victim to frostbite and he may lose his feet. Con-
versely, if his squad has made a fire, or he stands too close
to the stove in the warm-up tents that will soon be invented, the rubber will heat up quickly. His cold feet are
now gripped in a white-hot vise. And should he attempt
to warm his hands too quickly by a fire, the pain can become unbearable. Strong as he is, courageous as he has
shown himself, he will scream aloud.

A man must be careful not to sweat too much. He will
freeze to death in his own sweat. If he is working on an
emplacement, he will gradually remove his clothing in
layers—just as carefully restoring them when he has
finished. Marines climbing hills, Marines fighting, Marines

carrying their wounded buddies to safety or recovering their bodies—these Marines cannot tarry for such luxurious precaution and must pray for and await the warmth of dawn to dry them out.

"Dear God, give me tomorrow," they will pray, and then, if they have lived to see it, they will hasten to the warm-up tent or squat on the snow-swept slopes to remove the extra socks that have been drying against their flesh. They will exchange these for the sodden ones, after having rubbed their feet, and, if there is time, crawl into the sleeping bags that they must always carry. But they will not crawl completely in. Men surprised in their sleeping bags never live.

More than normally, men living in such cold must eat. But food freezes. There is usually a pot of hot water in the warm-up tent. Snow is melted and boiled on a stove stoked with wood torn from bombed Korean huts, or with oil to which gasoline has been added to make it burn. Powdered coffee from a man's rations may be mixed with this water. But it must be drunk quickly, for water freezes within eight feet of the stove. C rations—little cans of meat and beans, meat hash, meat stew—may be pitched into the pot to thaw. But only the outer parts thaw. A hard core of frozen food remains within. And yet, a hungry man will say, "Screw it, I'm starving," and devour that icy ball. And he will get enteritis, experience a terrible gnawing pain in the pit of his stomach—or, worse, he will get diarrhea. When the sudden pains of diarrhea stab his bowels, if he is luckily not fighting, he will bolt for the head, struggling with those layers of clothing. He will stop with a cry of anguish. He will stand there, soiled, sobs of helpless rage racking his body, the tears of loathing streaming down his cheeks and freezing there. He will remain this way, frozen in his own filth, until he can find a warm-up tent.

A fortunate man may find some chocolate or gumdrops in his ration. This is candy, sugar, good—full of quick energy. He pops it into his mouth, holding it against the palate with the tongue until it softens and can be chewed. This is how men slake their thirst: eating snow after canteens have frozen and burst. And crackers from the C ration may also be thawed in that single place of warmth within those frozen hills—the living human mouth.

In such cold, human blood also freezes, and plasma is useless. It is true that the cold may help a wounded man by stopping the flow of blood. But should he lie too long with torn and bloody flesh exposed, it may become blackened, and then doctors will turn sorrowing eyes away from the sight of the thin greenish fluid that marks gangrene. In tents pitched behind the lines, guarded by outposts of riflemen, these doctors may pause to scrape at blood that has frozen and caked on their gloves. Navy medical corpsmen will roam the lines, their mouths stuffed with thawing syrettes of morphine.

This is the cold that closed upon the First Marine Division marching up The Road, and this is the winter that laid a concealing cloak of blizzards and dark nights over the valleys and draws down which one hundred thousand Chinese came stealing—hiding by day in caves, mine shafts, and native huts, moving by night—gathering undetected in the positions from which they would spring the trap that would carry out their mission, the annihilation of the American Marines.

CHAPTER FOUR

THE United States Marines had yet to fight Chinese soldiers. The Chinese they had defeated in the Boxer Rebellion of 1900 were an untrained rabble. But the men massing secretly above them were something different, something new in modern history: They were trained Chinese soldiers with a tradition of victory.

Most of them were peasants from North China, sturdy and stoical youths in their teens and early twenties. Many had been torn from home and family upon reaching the military age of fifteen. To these were added a heavy leavening of the professionals who had served under the vanished Chinese war lords, or those Nationalists who had gone over to the Reds with the defeat of Chiang Kai-shek. Others were old-timers who had fought the war lords, the Japanese, and Chiang, and who still fought for Mao Tse-tung —for in the Chinese Communist Forces there is no retirement save death or disability.

They sprang from the new China, in which it was no longer fashionable to quote the sneering proverb, "As you do not use good metal for nails, so you do not use good men for soldiers." In the new China, which was the creation of those battle-scarred veterans who made the Long March, all the good metal and all the good men went into the army. Conscripts were fed an endless diet of Communist doctrine, digesting as much of it as their one to four years of formal education might allow, or as much as any foot soldier in ranks for life will really care about. During a minimum average of two years' training, these men of the Ninth Army Group were taught that inflexible obedience to orders, that willingness to charge an enemy position which American writers in heated editorial rooms derided as "blind fanaticism," but which their sons in Korea, unable to disqualify it with an epithet, were forced to regard as bravery.

The Chinese soldier possessed two qualities which at least counterbalanced a very poor supply system, a lack of artillery, and a confusing multiplicity of weapons of Russian, English, Japanese, and American make. These were the ability to suffer great hardship matched by the capacity to march and fight on small rations. Each of these Chinese soldiers carried five days' food in a cloth roll looped over his shoulder. It contained either rice from home or the Korean staple of millet seed, rice, and dried peas ground into a powder, which he cooks himself. If he can make no fire, he mixes it with water and eats it.

In winter the Chinese foot-slogger wears a heavy quilted cotton uniform over his summer dress. Outside it is mustard color, like a manila envelope. Inside it is white, and is often reversed for fighting in the snow. He has no helmet, only a heavy cotton cap with big earflaps and a neckpiece. His shoes are rubber or canvas sneakers fitted over layers of cotton socks.

In attack, these men preferred night fighting. They had no stomach for the daylight battle, during which

American air and artillery could cut them to bits. Their
tactics were to crawl toward the enemy positions under
cover of darkness. Then, to the blare of bugles, the shrilling
of whistles, the clanging of cymbals, they would leap to
their feet and charge. They wanted to get in close, depend-
ing on bayonets and those "potato masher" concussion
grenades which they primed by tapping on rocks or rifle
butts. They tried to turn the flanks, or to infiltrate, hoping
to gain the rear and then isolate small unit by small unit
which could then be chopped up piecemeal. Their commanders considered a three-to-one superiority ideal for
attack, though they did not use those "human sea" assaults of which some headline writers were so fond, and
which led one anonymous Marine to make the immortal
wisecrack: "Hey, Sarge—how many hordes in a Chinese
platoon?"

The men who led these new Chinese soldiers were among
the world's most experienced commanders. Some of them
had been handling troops since World War I and were
veterans of scores of battles. They knew "the book," too,
not merely those hard lessons they had learned in three
decades of guerrilla fighting. General Lin Pao, commander
of the 124th Division, had never known defeat. General
Sung Shin-lun, who led the Ninth Army Group, had been
handling men in combat since his graduation from
Whampoa Military Academy at the age of seventeen. Now,
at forty, a man who had commanded a regiment on the
Long March, General Sung was renowned for his mastery
of guerrilla warfare, for his bravery in battle—and for
his terrible temper.

It was Sung who had brought his hundred thousand
down to the Yalu by forced marches when the First Marine
Division was slicing northward. He took them over the

river at night and then led them 150 miles over mountainous terrain in a period of twelve days. Sung would earn
even the Marines' respect by striking them hard at a half-
dozen points along The Road within the space of a few
nights, springing his trap with a precision that was master-
ful. And he would attempt to inflame the battle ardor of
his troops by circulating a Russian naval captain's
pamphlet describing the hateful Marines they were about
to meet. The pamphlet began:

> When in the summer of 1950 the American im-
> perialist marauders, the newly appeared pretenders
> to world domination, provoked the bloody holocaust
> in Korea, the Wall Street house-dog General Mac-
> Arthur demanded that the American so-called
> "Marines" be immediately placed at his disposal.
> This professional murderer and inveterate war crimi-
> nal intended to throw them into battle as quickly as
> possible for the purpose of inflicting, as it seemed to
> him then, a final blow on the Korean people.
>
> In putting forward such a demand, MacArthur
> proceeded from the fact that U.S. "Marine" units
> have been trained more than any other types of
> American forces for the waging of the unprece-
> dentedly brutal and inhuman, predatory war against
> the freedom-loving, heroic Korean people.
>
> It was precisely to U.S. Marines that the Ober-
> bandit MacArthur addressed the words: "A rich city
> lies ahead of you, it has much wine and tasty morsels
> Take Seoul and all the girls will be yours, the prop-
> erty of the inhabitants belongs to the conquerors and
> you will be able to send parcels home."
>
> The events in Korea have shown graphically that

the Marine Corps stalwarts did not turn a deaf ear
to the appeal of their rapacious ataman. They have
abundantly covered Korean soil with the blood and
tears of hundreds and thousands of Korean women,
old people and children . . .

There were many more paragraphs, equally appetizing,
and once the men had swallowed the Russian pamphleteer's
main course, it was General Sung himself who served
dessert with this eve-of-battle harangue: "Soon we will
meet the American Marines in battle. We will destroy
them. When they are defeated the enemy army will collapse
and our country will be free from the threat of aggression.
Kill these Marines as you would snakes in your homes."

Plainly, General Sung Shin-lun and his hundred
thousand had marched down the mountains for nothing
less than annihilation of the men of the First Marine
Division.

And who were they?

CHAPTER FIVE

THEY were the Old Breed and the New Breed.

The Old: noncoms and officers of every rank who had fought the Division's battles at Guadalcanal, New Britain, Peleliu, Okinawa . . . or had been with the Second at Tarawa, the Third at Iwo Jima . . . at Bougainville . . . Saipan, Guam . . . at a dozen other battlefields . . . or in the skies above Midway, the Solomons . . . manning Naval guns in the Coral Sea, off Leyte Gulf . . . They could load jeeps with their decorations, would need a truck to carry off their Purple Hearts.

And the New: bright-eyed youngsters who had come in after World War II, and had stayed . . . the teen-agers marking time in the Marines until their military service was done and they might go off to jobs or college . . . and the Reservists, those civilians who spent a few nights a month drilling in armories, two weeks at summer camp, thereby earning a couple of extra dollars and the right to wear the uniform—until Korea came and they were in "for the duration" . . . The Reservists had their sprinkling of Old Breed, too, but they had grown soft in offices and factories, had families to worry about and ranch houses to pay for . . . Even they could not escape the stinging taunt which the Old Breed gives the New! "Sonny, I've worn out more sea bags than you have socks."

But they met and merged, the Old and the New, in the crucible of Pusan and the Naktong River. When they swept ashore at Inchon they were just that single breed of American Marine—the "Jarheads," as the swab-jockies called them in this brand-new war. When they hit Seoul, it is doubtful if America ever before possessed a striking force so seasoned and so battlewise in every rank from commanding general to the private with the rifle in his hand and the grenade on his belt. Twenty-five thousand men, and very few of them without a battle star.

Among those men who took The Road to Yudam-ni, the Reservoir, and the trap, was Staff Sergeant Robert Kennemore. Serious, tough-minded, and soft-voiced and careful in speech, Kennemore at twenty-nine had passed through a lifetime of adversity. At fourteen he ran away from his home in Greenville, South Carolina, unable to endure the hell-fire-and-damnation preaching of a stern stepfather. He worked his way north, then west, stopping in Chicago to put himself through night high school while he worked by day. In 1940, he became a Marine in time to fight at Guadalcanal as a corporal. In November 1950, Sergeant Kennemore was a professional, proud of that hard calling that had firmed his mouth and sunk the hollows beneath his cheekbones.

In Kennemore's machine-gun section were Privates Tom Gallagher from Boston and Ezekiel Jones of Alabama. Gallagher was one of those youngsters caught in the Marines when war came. He was short, stocky, swarthy. He was impudent and cared little for the niceties of rank. But if his tongue was saucy, he had an admirable habit of

pulling stunts in combat that were not "out of the book."
Kennemore wouldn't trade Ezekiel for another set of guns.
Ezekiel could make you laugh, even in this miserable cold.
Moving up The Road, he had come to Kennemore with a
worried frown on his face.

"Sarge, they ain't no snakes up there, is they?"

"I dunno, Zeke. Why, you scared of snakes?"

"Me: Scared? Hell's fire, Sarge, I ain't scared o' no
snakes 'ceptin' big ones, little ones, live ones, and dead
ones!"

So they laugh and trudge on, forgetting for a moment
the numbness in their feet.

And behind them, marching in a rifle company, comes a
giant of a man named Hector Cafferata. He stands nearly
six feet four inches. He weighs 235 pounds, battle-trimmed
though he might be. He dwarfs his buddy, Pfc. Ken Benson
—a blond, square-faced youth of eighteen who is merely
six feet tall, 200 pounds in weight. Cafferata is nineteen.
Back home in Boonton, New Jersey, he had been a star
semipro football player. He had been a great hunter,
roaming the Jersey hills with a rifle in his hands since the
age of nine. He had been planning to get married, but
a friend had persuaded him to rejoin a Reserve unit the
very night it shoved off. Now that friend marches with him.

"Goddamit, Bens, I shoulda never listened to ya. Valley
Forge was a cookout compared to this place."

"Blow it, will ya? Nobody twisted yer arm. Anyway,
where's the gumdrops? We got gumdrops in the ration
today and I get the gumdrops."

"All right, ya pack rat. But, remember—when we get
the rations with chocolate in 'em, I get the chocolate."

They march on. Thawing in Benson's mouth are the

gumdrops. He would like to curse about being issued stones for food, but it's much more sensible to save your breath for walking.

These were the men, multiplied by thousands—kids named Smith, Pomers, O'Leary, Robinson—and ahead of them were their junior officers. Captain Sam Jaskilka was a veteran who marched wondering if his orders for a transfer stateside had gone through.

Lieutenant John Yancey worried about the new baby born the day he had landed at Inchon or fretted about the liquor store he had left behind in Little Rock, Arkansas. Here he was, a Navy Cross veteran of Guadalcanal, a man who had eaten Okinawa mud, called back from the Reserves to do it again.

Joe (the Bull) Fisher had a company, though he was only a first lieutenant. But he was a pro, and he had been chosen over captains because the Bull loved to lead and fight. Six feet, 220 pounds, able to fortify his authority with his fists, Fisher yet possessed a deep contempt for bullies. He led by example.

Captain William Barber had only recently taken charge of Fox Company, Seventh, and had celebrated the occasion by breaking out the men and telling them to shave, to clean their weapons, to cut the comedy and knock off the scuttlebutt about being home for Christmas. And he had grinned to hear them grumble, for Barber knew that gum-beating Marines are hard to lick. He knew, because he had beat his chops in ranks himself, had spent his first two years as an enlisted paratrooper before he won his Silver Star and Purple Heart on Iwo for rescuing two wounded Marines under fire. Barber was a "mustang," an officer up

from the ranks. There were many more of that hard
breed—commanders who had first learned to obey—moving
up The Road.

Commanding the First Regiment was perhaps the most
famous Marine of all time—the celebrated Colonel Lewis
(Chesty) Puller. Here was a professional whose career
ran back to World War I—who had fought in Haiti,
Nicaragua, across the Pacific, had wrested Seoul from the
Reds. Chesty of the enormous rib cage supported by a pair
of spindly sticks for legs—five feet six inches tall and much
of that height occupied by a commanding head and out-
thrust jaw. He held five Navy Crosses, more than any
other American living or dead. He numbered his battles by
the score. His creed was attack and he boasted that he had
never commanded an office in Washington. Here was a
mustang who was a living legend to Marines, whose deeds
in battle were rivaled only by his wisecracks. When he
saw his first flame-thrower: "Where do you put the bayonet
on it?" When a battalion commander before Bloody Nose
Ridge on Peleliu reported he hadn't enough men to hold:
"What d'ya mean not enough to hold? You there, ain't
you, colonel?" When he spoke to his officers before Seoul:
"It's about time we got off our dead asses and earned our
pay." And then, reflecting his deep faith in the men he
led, when General MacArthur reminded him that the corps
of Red cadets in Seoul might do to him what the cadets of
V.M.I. did to the Union's General Hunter in the Civil
War: "Mebbe so, General, but Hunter wasn't leading
Marines." That was Puller, flamboyant, cocky, combative
—and yet a man who never stopped studying the military
art or reading history.

"Blitzin' Litzen" commanded the Seventh. Colonel
Homer L. Litzenberg had been a boot himself, had had

his head shaved clean at Parris Island in 1922, had pulled
mess duty or swabbed out the head with a squeegee. Stocky,
square-faced, bred in the Pennsylvania steel country,
Litzenberg was a man whose outer toughness masked a
deep inner passion. He could be moved to tears by tales
of the valor or suffering of his men. He was also good-
natured. Many an officer of equal rank would be astonished
to see how lightly he regarded the ribbing of his staff,
or when his unit was off the lines, how eagerly he would sit
down to drink and sing with them. Litzenberg had much
sea duty behind him, and his share of decorations. He was
one of the few Marines who had seen European service in
World War II, though he had also fought in the Pacific.
Here was a mustang who had been inside many military
classrooms and who had made plans for the Joint Chiefs
of Staff. "Blitzin' Litzen" they called him because his
battle tactics yoked caution to combativeness. He would
mark his foe first, be sure of him, and then overwhelm
him.

There was a "light colonel" leading the Fifth—that
famous, arrogant regiment which had been born in Belleau
Wood, had won the French *fourragère* for its charge there,
and had never, as the men of the First and Seventh will tell
you, got over it. Yet it was a tribute to Lieutenant Colonel
Raymond L. Murray that he should be left in command
of such a regiment with no more than a light colonel's silver
leaves on his shoulders. There were many full colonels in
the First Marine Division, but Murray still led the Fifth.
He was thirty-seven. He was tall, broad-shouldered, raw-
boned, with a fighting, angular face. He was no mustang,
but another breed of Marine commander: one of those who
study in military schools other than Annapolis and West
Point and come into the Marines. Texas A & M had given

him his military studies, and Peking and Iceland had
proved his capacity to lead. He had studied again at the
British Force Tactical School, and then at twenty-nine
had commanded a battalion on Guadalcanal. He was still
commanding it at Tarawa, and again at Saipan where,
with two Silver Stars to his credit, he won his Navy Cross
for holding that battered unit together though seriously
wounded himself. Murray was highly regarded as a
planner as well as a field leader, and his great personal
bravery was complemented by a simple clarity of speech
which made his orders and his reasons plain.

These were the men and the commanders moving up The
Road. And who commanded them?

His name was Smith.

Major General Oliver P. Smith was an original among
Marines. He didn't drink. He never swore. In moments
of stress or excitement, he pulled mildly at a short pipe.
Yet Oliver Smith always seemed able to find a drink for
a man who thought he needed one, nor was he ever more
than amused by the fiery language of the Marines around
him. And the troops always got their smokes.

At fifty-seven Oliver Smith still had a full head of hair.
It was pure white. The blue eyes beneath it were mild. In
greeting, his broad mouth usually parted in a warm smile.
Only the erectness of his slender six-foot frame seemed to
mark his craft. He was a scholar, a reader whose library
was loaded with novels as well as with histories and military
texts. When he had come into the Marines as a lieutenant
in May 1917, he was already a master of shorthand. He
developed the habit of noting down all that was said at
conferences, of quickly transcribing his notes, of keeping
voluminous records. At the Army's Infantry School at
Fort Benning, at the French War College, at the Marine

Corps Schools in Quantico, Oliver Smith showed himself
to be one of those rare men who love to work and who
find a natural delight in detail. But General Smith had
also led in battle. He had commanded the Fifth at Talasea
on New Britain, had been assistant division commander
at Peleliu and the Tenth Army's Marine deputy chief
of staff at Okinawa. Though a born planner, he could
realize that men and munitions move on earth as well as
on paper. He studied his men and treated each according
to his character. During the awful slaughter of Peleliu,
he had come ashore seeking the tempestuous commander
of the First Regiment—Chesty Puller. Finding him in a
typically profane rage at a typical cannon's mouth command post, he could admonish him gently: "Now, Louie,
you know you needn't get up this close."

When in command, Oliver Smith acted on two simple
principles. The first was to be prepared for the worst,
the second to be optimistic when it came.

It was the first rule that concerned him as Litzenberg's
Seventh Regiment took The Road from Hamhung to the
Reservoir. He was alarmed to see his First Marine Division
strung out in bits, battalion by battalion, from south to
north. They would reach a point where as much as 175
miles separated his southernmost and northernmost units.
And the cold was socking in. So General Smith protested
to Major General Edward Almond, commander of the
Tenth Corps. But to no avail. Wasn't it merely a matter
of mopping up the routed North Koreans?

Then the Seventh had run into the Chinese. At Sudong
in early November, Blitzin' Litzen had chewed up the
Chinese 124th Division, handing General Lin Pao his first
defeat. The Chinese had scurried north, and to Smith
it was plain that they had been stationed below Koto merely

to delay the Marines while something stronger was being prepared at the Reservoir. He had brought a Chinese prisoner down to the port of Hungnam to show him to the Secretary of the Navy who had flown in from the States.

Well, yes, the man was decidedly a Chinese, but probably one of those "volunteers" the Communists had been feeding into North Korea. At the highest levels of General MacArthur's command, the word was still: "The Chinese won't come in."

Now alarmed, General Smith wrote to Marine Commandant Clifton B. Cates in Washington: "I do not like the prospect of stringing out a Marine division along a single mountain road from Hamhung to the border . . ."

Then, fearing the worst, Smith acted. He fought to bring his units closer together. He approached Tenth Corps with a proposition to build an airport on the plateau at Hagaru, midway between Hamhung and the Reservoir.

"We are going to need a place for supply and the evacuation of casualties."

Came the answer: "What casualties?"

Smith did not argue. He obtained permission to go ahead with the airfield himself, though such construction was the function of a corps, not a division. On November 16, a helmet jammed over his mane of white hair, pipe in mouth, General Smith entered a heated station wagon and drove up the winding road to Hagaru. Midway he overtook an open jeep carrying Major General Field Harris, the commander of the First Marine Air Wing. General Harris, having forgotten to reckon with the weather, was blue with cold. Grinning, Smith ordered his driver to halt.

"Like a ride, General?"

Harris's reply was to clamber from his open vehicle and

hobble on numbed feet to the station wagon. He climbed in.

"Goddam! This is more like it. Got another one of these wagons, O. P.?"

"Well, yes," Smith said reluctantly.

"How about it?"

"Well, yes," Smith repeated, sadly reflecting upon the lengths to which Good Samaratanism may force a man. "You can pick it up when we get back." And yet General Smith would shortly discover that a heated station wagon was a small favor to grant the man whose First Marine Air Wing would do more to save his First Marine Division from annihilation than any other unit in Korea.

The two generals drove on to Hagaru. They alighted at the village and set out over the frozen ground, hunting for an airfield site. They found it in a bean field to the south of both The Road and the town.

"It'd be a bog in the summer," Smith muttered, stamping the rocklike earth. "But this is one break we get from the winter. It's frozen solid."

General Harris agreed, certain that they could build a strip long enough to receive C-47s, those two-engine work horses of the Air Force Combat Cargo Command. They turned around and drove back to Hamhung, Harris to pick up his station wagon, Smith to locate Lieutenant Colonel John H. Partridge of the First Division's engineers. Three days later, Partridge's men came up The Road and were at work with bulldozers and earth movers. The frozen hills echoed to the whining of the dozers and shook to the blast of explosives loosening the earth.

The airfield was begun.

CHAPTER SIX

COLONEL LITZENBERG and his men couldn't be-
lieve it. How could ordinary Chinese soldiers know the complete plan of battle for a full army group? What
Intelligence was saying just wasn't possible. But there it
was: captured Chinese soldiers had volunteered the information that a huge force was gathering to the north in the
vicinity of Chosin Reservoir. This force, the Ninth Army
Group, was planning to allow the two leading regiments of
the First Marine Division to pass into the rugged mountain
country to the left and above the Reservoir at Yudam-ni.
When they had gone far enough, the Chinese would strike
them hard, cut them off, annihilate them—and then roll
over the remaining Marines at Hagaru and Koto before
falling upon the rest of Tenth Corps to drive it into the
sea at Hungnam.

It was fantastic. Not the plan, of course—that seemed
to fit the situation very well. For it was true that the
Seventh and the Fifth Regiments were going to attack to
the left from Yudam-ni on the afternoon of November 27.
The Fifth would move through the Seventh, marching from
the right side of the Reservoir after being relieved by one

field artillery and two infantry battalions of the Army's Seventh Division. This was the unit that would be known as Task Force Faith, after Lieutenant Colonel Don C. Faith, its ultimate commander.

No, thought Colonel Litzenberg, there's nothing screwy about the *plan*. But how in the name of God would two Chinese peasant soldiers know it in the detail usually reserved for Marine colonels? He lifted his shoulders helplessly. The only thing to do was to become wary—and send the report along to Division.

General Smith saw it, and once again became concerned. Something was brewing. Worse, since November 25 all the news had been bad. That was the day the Communist Chinese had shown that they were "coming in"—and coming in with a savage rush. Already, the Eighth Army on the left was reeling backward. A gap of eighty miles lay between them and the Marines on their right. Wouldn't it be foolish to assume that no one was in that gap?

But the orders for the division to attack still held. The Fifth would be jumping off on the 27th. There was nothing to do but mark time, to be thankful that the airstrip at Hagaru would soon receive planes, that Puller's First would soon have a battalion there, as well as a battalion below at Koto, and still farther down at Chinhung-ni, another battalion. If worst came to worst, as Smith now fully expected, he would have a plan. Somehow, The Road would have to be kept open.

Lieutenant Colonel Murray didn't like it. Upon his arrival at Yudam-ni, Litzenberg had told him of the Intelligence report, and also expressed concern at the stiffening resistance he had met along The Road from Hagaru. And, now, on the afternoon of the 27th, Murray's Second Battalion under Lieutenant Colonel Harold Roise was running into something more than "stiffening resistance." Not a quarter mile out in the hills, the Marines had been hit by mortars and intense small-arms fire. There had been roadblocks. The enemy—and it was definitely a Chinese enemy—was dug in on the ridge slopes. Even the help of Marine air, Corsairs diving to strafe and bomb, had not flushed them out. Roise had not gone two thousand yards when Murray pulled him back. It was getting close to dusk. The Marines were climbing hills, digging in for the night, setting up battalion perimeters, cursing with bitter anger at the frail entrenching tools snapping in their hands.

Casualties had already begun to pile up in the valley that was Yudam-ni. These were the wounded from Litzen-berg's march, from the Fifth's day of fighting. And already there were the casualties from the cold—the men who were "shook," who had suddenly passed from a state of numbed shock into uncontrollable sobbing. True, most of these had recovered and returned to the lines, but there were still a few of them lying within the slowly darkening tents, along with the men who had been careless enough to let the sweat ice too firmly within their shoe-pacs. Corpsmen moved among them, lighting candles in the dark.

Lieutenant Colonel Olin Beall's First Motor Transport Battalion had put in a good day's work. Since dawn the drivers had been bringing their supply-laden trucks into Yudam-ni from Hagaru. There was now plenty of ammunition, enough shells to keep most of the guns of the Eleventh, the Division's artillery regiment, blasting away during a prolonged battle. There were other units of the Eleventh down at Hagaru, and they could fire north. But most of the 105's, and some of the 155 howitzers were emplaced around the village.

Just before dusk, Beall's motor-men turned their empty trucks around preparatory to a quick run back to Hagaru. Beall knew there had been enemy movement in the hills bordering The Road between the two towns, but he thought his trucks could run the gantlet.

It was not yet dark when Pfc. Charles Kaylor was called to the tent of Second Lieutenant Nicholas Kavakich.

"Kaylor, your request for release from active duty has been approved. Here's the orders, and if you want to get the hell out of here, you'd better hurry."

Kaylor hurried. He whirled, without a moment wasted on happy exclamation, and dashed back to his machine-gun section. He gathered his gear while his astonished buddies crowded around him. They jawed at him.

"Beat 'em, boys, beat 'em till they're sore," he replied cheerfully. "Private First Class Kaylor is goin' home for Christmas."

"I'm a son of a bitch! How'd you do it?"

"Easy, boys, I'm just a writer among fighters. I wrote the Commandant that I had two kids and a business. So I'm goin' home."

"An' that was *my* pen you used, you one-way—"

"Thanks, ol' buddy—I'll send you a turkey wing."

But Pfc. Kaylor did share out his candy and cigarettes before he shouted his last good-bys, turned and ran off to overtake one of the last of Beall's trucks moving down a hill to gain The Road.

He was going home to Minneapolis.

From time to time during the late afternoon, Staff Sergeant Robert Kennemore and Private Tom Gallagher of Easy Company, Seventh, had left off digging in their machine guns atop North Ridge, a hill to the east of The Road and about 600 yards above the Fifth and Seventh Regimental command posts in Yudam-ni. The two men stopped to gaze glumly at the trucks whinning out of town and south to Hagaru. They thought they carried the soldiers of Task Force Faith who were in position on the right side of the Reservoir.

"I told you this war was just about over, Sarge," Gallagher growled. "And who's gonna be the first ones home for Christmas? The goddam dogfaces!"

"You know it," Kennemore murmured. "C'mon, let's get that second gun in. It's getting dark."

Gallagher did not answer. He had suddenly tensed. He was staring at something he had seen to the front of the machine-gun positions.

"Goddam, Sarge," he said softly. "There's a Chink out there." He seized his rifle and started slipping down the hill. "An' I'm gonna get him."

Before Kennemore could restrain him, Gallagher was gone.

There was a shot.

The Marines scrambled for their guns.

Gallagher reappeared.

"Hey, Sarge," he yelled. "He musta been an officer. He had a dispatch case."

Lieutenant Ray Ball, Easy's executive officer, came running over to join Gallagher and Kennemore in going through the dead man's carrying case. They found a plotting board, an alidade, and a tape measure—all probably used in diagraming the Marine positions.

"Thorough bastard, wasn't he?" Lieutenant Ball mused. But there was no mirth in his eyes, nor in anyone else's. They were wary. Silently, moved by a single thought, the three men turned to gaze behind and below them at the supplies and wounded and headquarters tents lying 600 yards to the south in Yudam-ni. They did not speak. They knew the spot they were in.

Toktong Pass had to be held.

It threaded steep ridges midway between Yudam-ni and Hagaru. It was roughly seven miles equidistant from both. Whoever commanded Toktong Pass ruled The Road in either direction—north to reinforce, south to retreat.

On the morning of the 27th, Captain William Barber received orders to take his Fox Company, Seventh, from Hagaru to Toktong. Being a methodical man, Barber collected his platoon leaders and drove north in a jeep to go over the ground himself. He chose a high hill mass standing above the pass. On this height he could look down the throats of anyone trying to force The Road.

He returned to Hagaru where his men were gathered, grumbling, cursing the cold with a bitterness usually reserved for their commanders, stamping their feet, or crowding about tiny wood fires for warmth. One of them, a sergeant, had been rereading his "Dear John" letter—those infamous missives which unfaithful wives sometimes send their fighting husbands, and which often begin: "It pains me to tell you this, but while you have been gone, I have been seeing an old high school friend . . ."

The sergeant scowled. There was no longer any sardonic humor in the letter. His buddies had long since wrung it dry of laughs, though they still called him "Sergeant Dee-

Jay" in its memory. Sergeant Dee-Jay made up his mind. He walked over to Private Cafferata.

"Listen," he growled, "I've had it. I'm getting the hell out of here."

"Sure, Sarge," Cafferata said. "I'll call you a cab."

"Cut the crap. I mean it! This goddam war's just about over. They don't need me no more. An' my old woman ain't getting rid of me so easy."

"So whaddaya want from me?"

"Shoot me."

Astonishment rippled across Cafferata's pugnacious features. Then they crinkled in amusement.

"You popped yer cork or somethin', Sarge?"

"C'mon, Moose," the sergeant pleaded. "Shoot me. Lemme have it in the arm and we can say it's an accident. It ain't as though we was in combat. Yuh know this screwy war's over. C'mon, shoot me."

Cafferata shook his head wonderingly. "Yer off yer rocker, Sarge. Yuh know damn well they'd just patch yuh up and send yuh back to duty. Yuh wanna get stateside, yuh gotta be carried out." He hefted his rifle and grinned. "I could shoot yuh inna leg, break the bone."

Sergeant Dee-Jay winced. "Nah. That'd hurt too much."

Cafferata pondered. "I could knock yuh out an' then break yer arm with my rifle butt."

"Yuh mean hit me?"

"Nah. You just hold yer breath and I'll squeeze yuh."

The sergeant reflected. He glanced at the letter in his hand. "C'mon," he said.

Cafferata flexed his powerful arms and shoulders. The sergeant took three deep breaths. Cafferata wrapped his arms around his middle and squeezed. The sergeant passed out. Cafferata carefully arranged the sergeant's left arm against the snow. He clubbed his rifle and struck.

Whack!

He stepped back. Benson and a few others crowded around. Sergeant Dee-Jay's eyelids fluttered. He came to. He lifted his injured arm, and an expression that was the perfection of anguish came over his face.

"Yuh clumsy son of a bitch!" he wailed. "Yuh didn't break it!"

Cafferata flushed. "It ain't my fault," he mumbled. " 'At goddam parka's got too much padding in it. Roll it up."

"An' get frostbite?" the sergeant screamed.

"Awright, awright—let's try again."

The sergeant arose. He drew breath again. Again Cafferata squeezed, again the sergeant sank to the ground, again the blow fell.

And again the sergeant's eyes opened and his voice broke in a fury of frustration. "It ain't broken! Yuh shoe-making son of a bitch, yuh didn't bust it!"

Now Cafferata was nettled. Doubt had been cast upon his great strength. For the third time he squeezed. For the third time the sergeant lay supine. But now, Cafferata was neatly propping the outflung arm against a log, and was backing off for the stroke—and then the voice of authority sliced sharply across that pregnant silence.

"What in hell's going on here?"

It was the platoon leader.

Swiftly, with the concerted, practiced ease of men in ranks, the voices rose in a chorus of lies.

"Nothin', sir."

"The sarge slipped and fell."

"He passed out."

"He's shook, sir."

"We was givin' him air."

Red-faced, Sergeant Dee-Jay arose. The platoon leader glared helplessly. "Well, you'd better damn well get your breath back fast. We're moving out!"

"Where, sir?"

"Up north."

So they fell in, the aggrieved Sergeant Dee-Jay among them, his arm as sore as his heart, and they clambered aboard the trucks that would take them up The Road to a place called Toktong Pass.

There is no record of what General Sung Shin-lun said —if he said anything—when he learned on that late afternoon of November 27 that his victims had not poked their heads too deeply into his trap. In his headquarters ten miles north of Yudam-ni, he must have received word that the Fifth had pulled back and that both Marine regiments were digging in. He knew, too, that Fox Company had occupied the hill that was to bear its name. He was aware that Hagaru contained that priceless airstrip and that it had only been recently reinforced. But he would attend to Hagaru another night.

Tonight, for the opening blows in his offensive of annihilation, he would concentrate on at least surrounding Yudam-ni, obliterating the unknown force atop Fox Hill and cutting The Road in as many places as possible by seizing high ground to cover roadblocks. Then he would have them—and the rest of the division would fall to him like rotten fruit.

At dark, under orders from General Sung's division leaders, the soldiers of the Ninth Army Group crept from their village huts, their caves, and mine shafts and padded silently into position. They came over frozen streams, along ridge sides, down draws. They were very cold. The area which the enemy Marines called "Frozen Chosin" had been no kinder to them—had been worse, in fact, their feet being shod as they were in canvas and rubber. Sometimes, when they lay down to squirm forward toward a position, a few of them would not move. No one bothered to kick them or beat them. It was obvious that they were frozen where they lay.

But they came forward, the grenadiers moving out first to be within throwing distance when the first bugle blared, the first cymbal clanged—and Chinese soldiers would grapple with American Marines.

CHAPTER SEVEN

IT WAS about nine o'clock on the night of November 27. But Sergeant Kennemore was still awake, twisting about in his sleeping bag for warmth. His empty belly growled angrily. He sat upright and fumbled for a can of meat and beans, and opened it. He stabbed at the frozen mess with his bayonet point, seeking to soften it, make it edible. But he only chipped it. Infuriated, he flung it from him. The can struck that iron ground with a metallic clank.

"Whassat?" one of the men in front cried, tension stringing his voice taut.

"Nothing. It's me. Kennemore. I dropped a can."

Sergeant Kennemore lay back. He doubted if he would sleep, and he felt a bitterness deep enough to taste rising sourly within him. What the hell kind of a war was this? A paper-assed "police action," with the people at home not caring a damn. He huddled in his bag, shivering as the cold, already falling to 20 degrees below zero, iced his flesh and froze his feet into lumps of pain. He'd better try to sleep. He'd have to be on watch soon.

Sergeant Kennemore dozed off.

It was getting on toward nine, but Captain Sam Jaskilka still fortified himself against the cold by anticipation of the daylight that would mean departure for him. Tomorrow he'd be shoving off. He hoped to be home before his wife, Norma, had the baby. And he was jubilant, hardly conscious of the cold except as a background of dark discomfort against which his good fortune might shine more brightly.

Perhaps the Chinese might come tonight, as everyone seemed to expect. But Jaskilka's Easy Company, Fifth, would be ready for them. Just before dark, Captain Sam had made his last tour of battle lines in Korea. His company held the center of Northwest Ridge, which stood about 2,000 yards northwest of the Fifth and Seventh command posts. Jaskilka had been especially pleased with Lieutenant Jack Nolan's disposition of a platoon of riflemen and machine gunners in difficult terrain. Nolan's guns could rake the corridor which Easy Company had been assigned to protect. This was a low floor crossed by a frozen stream and dotted with native huts. Nolan's guns could tie in with those of Lieutenant Ed Deptula on the left. With mortars set up to the rear of both platoons, Chinese attempting to force the corridor in hopes of gaining Yudam-ni and The Road would have to move through a rain of fire.

So Captain Jaskilka had observed this and had gone back to his command post confident, even though Deptula had been hit by a stray bullet at dusk and had to be evacuated. Sergeant Russ Borgomaneiro who replaced him was an excellent noncom, and Jaskilka trusted him—as he trusted the Fox and Dog Companies, Fifth, holding down his left flank.

Let the Chinese come. They were ready. And there was always that wonderful tomorrow.

Sergeant Kennemore thought he heard music. He stirred in his sleeping bag. On the thin cold wind sweeping over him he seemed to hear the faint sound of bugles.

My God! They *were* bugles.

Sergeant Kennemore scrambled to his feet.

Lieutenant Yancey and Private Gallagher had been asking God to damn and blast that moon which had come over the mountain behind them, outlining them, when they, too, heard the bugles. Shadows were gliding over the ground toward them. Now the bugles were blaring in full voice, whistles were shrilling, the shadows were lowering, lengthening, a chant of voices was rising to a clamor:

> *Son of a bitch, Marines*
> *We kill—*
> *Son of a bitch, Marines*
> *You die.*

And then the Chinese hit the trip flares.

Up spurted the flame and light, and the shadows were men in white moving to the attack. Gallagher saw the first wave coming at a trot, firing as they came—behind them the second wave, grasping for grenades, the third, a fourth, men as far back as that eerie, gradually diminishing light could reach. Then the flares were out and only the moon was left to light the battlefield.

"Give it to the bastards!" Gallagher screamed, his voice drowned in the stuttering of his own machine gun, the pounding of the heavy to his right.

Now the general wail and confusion of battle was upon
them all. Chinese fell, but their ranks were quickly filled.
They kept trying to close, hurling their potato mashers.
Marines lobbed their own grenades. Hoarse death cries
rose in the night, beneath them the shriller screams of the
wounded. Frantically Yancey cranked up his telephone
and yelled to Lieutenant Ball with the mortars.

"Get those goddam mortars going!"

In came the 60mm's, flashing out of the tubes with a
metallic *plop*, thumping and crashing among the Chinese
—tearing and rending flesh. But the squat men in white
still bored in on North Ridge.

Yancey felt it difficult to breathe. He placed a finger
against his nose and felt the wet, tattered flesh where a
grenade fragment had lodged. He had to cough and spit
to get his breath. But he kept yelling to Ball for mortars,
shouting to his men, "Gung ho! Let's go! Gung ho! Let's
go!" It was a cry the realistic Yancey would normally
have despised as swashbuckling, but now it came breaking
from his tortured throat. And Gallagher was still firing.

Sergeant Kennemore was scrambling wildly down the
hill. He was making for one of his guns on the extreme
right, where most of the firing seemed to be centered. He
tried to fire his carbine as he ran. It fired a single round
and quit on automatic. It would only fire single shots. He
saw a figure coming up the hill.

The figure was scuttling, moving backward on the seat
of its pants, propelling itself with its hands, one leg
crumpled and useless before it. It was Easy Company's
commander, Captain Walter Phillips.

"Where you going?" Phillips cried.

"Down to the gun."

"Don't go down there, you damn fool! They've taken it.
They got me in the leg."

Kennemore paused. Below him, vaguely—he would never
be sure if he had actually seen it—he made out a crowd of
Chinese dragging the Marine machine gunner from his
hole, pulling him by the legs, bayoneting him, clubbing
him.

Kennemore fell on all fours and crawled to his left. He
came to his other gun. The gunner was on his knees, holding the gun in his hands, spraying with it.

"Grenades," someone called. "Get grenades!"

Kennemore squirmed on the hard ground. He crept
from body to body, Chinese or American, dead or wounded,
gathering grenades. He scurried back to the Marines still
firing, with rifles, with machine guns, with BARs. He
passed out grenades. Now the tap-tap of arming potato
mashers came from both sides as the Marines employed
the enemy's weapons.

Somehow, Sergeant Kennemore knew that Lieutenant
Ball was dead. Had he seen him killed alongside him? He
would never be sure. And Ezekiel Jones was hit. But
Kennemore had to get ammo for the machine guns. He
moved back and forth over that postage stamp of a
battlefield, supplying his men, shouting encouragement
to them.

The battle was hand to hand. Chinese were in on them.
They fought each other with knife and rifle butt, with
fists. The squat men were thrown back. Screaming, yelling,
cursing, and the banging of weapons filled Kennemore's
ears. The Chinese were throwing grenades. They were
landing in the snow around Kennemore and the others.
They landed, they lay there for an instant—or for an
eternity. They lay imbedded, framed in white, horrible

ugly things, dirty with death—and Kennemore stooped swiftly in that eternal instant to grasp them and hurl them back.

A potato masher plumped into the snow in front of him. It was too far to reach, no time to seize and throw . . . Kennemore put his left foot on it, stomping it into the snow. Another came in beside it. Staff Sergeant Kennemore dropped his knee upon it.

They exploded.

At ten o'clock Captain Sam Jaskilka gave up his wonderful tomorrow.

"Captain, this is Nolan. They're gathering in front of us. The place is crawling with them. Request illumination shells."

Jaskilka sighed, hung up the telephone, and tried to get battalion to fulfill Nolan's request. But there weren't enough of those 81mm shells to be spared. Jaskilka got back to Nolan and broke the bad news.

"Hold your fire till the last moment," he concluded.

Nolan waited. Borgomaneiro waited. Their men ran aching hands up and down their brittle rifle barrels, twiddled frozen trigger fingers for circulation, brushed aside the ice that had frozen on both sides of parka hoods.

Whistles sliced through the night. Bugles blatted.

Chinese grenadiers who had crawled forward leaped to their feet to throw their charges. Automatic rifles and machine guns opened up on the hills somewhere out in the black. Rifle fire raked the Marine lines on Northwest Ridge.

"Don't fire," Nolan whispered to the men near him. "Pass the word. They're feeling us out. They want us to give our positions away."

Bullets and grenades swept the men of Easy Company.

Then the mortars came raining in. Shells striking that unyielding earth, caught within that girdling amphitheater of hills, gave off a terrible crashing sound as though exploding within a huge basin of steel. Shell fragments flew. Rock fragments flew, clods of frozen earth. Marines drove their faces into the ground, grinding their teeth, struggling not to sob, feeling the rushing air knead and gouge them with giant fingers. They waited.

The mortars lifted, began walking toward the rear. They roved the lines of Dog and Fox Companies to the left. Jaskilka could see Fox Company's front flaming with shellfire.

Whistles shrieked again, and the enemy guns fell silent.

The Chinese charged.

They came on in columns, in whole squad formations, coming at that crazy trot—into the corridor that would be nicknamed Easy Alley for the windrows of enemy dead that would clog it. They came into the murderous interlocking fire of Nolan's and Borgomaneiro's guns and they fell in twos and in groups, sometimes in a squad line. Fox Company heaped them up, too. But they were many. Ultimately they burst the line between Fox and Easy. They poured into the gap, running into the rear with an aimless lack of purpose that startled some of the Marines who saw those dark shapes flying past. One Marine rifleman had pulled the pin of a hand grenade just as a Chinese flitted past him. He handed him the grenade. The enemy soldier seized it and dashed on. The Marine flung himself to the ground.

Wham!

Now groups of Chinese had the Marines' rear, threaten-

ing Lieutenant Colonel Roise's command post. He formed
a reserve of headquarters and service people. But he never
needed it. The Chinese failed to exploit their breakthrough.

Quickly Jaskilka sent his reserve platoon moving up to
the bulge. In total darkness, amid the din and confusion
of battle, Sergeant Borgomaneiro marshaled his reinforcements, redeployed his own men. And while Nolan skillfully
bent his lines back and leftward, Borgomaneiro's men contained the penetration. Those Chinese who had gotten
through died in individual combat, bayoneted for the most
part.

Still the Red commander stuffed that salient with troops.
But the Marines were in control. The enemy was cut down
systematically. A half-hour after the attack had begun,
Nolan received his "illumination." His gunners fired
tracers into the Korean huts, setting them on fire. The
Chinese were framed in the glare of the burning buildings,
trapped in the corridor, along the hills.

And they were slaughtered.

With the advent of dawn, some 700 enemy dead would
be heaped outside the lines of Roise's companies on Northwest Ridge—300 in front of Easy Company alone. Never
again would the Red commander try Easy Alley—and
many more cold dark nights would pass before Captain
Sam Jaskilka caught himself rejoicing over his lucky
transfer home.

To the right, on the hill where Sergeant Kennemore had
fallen, strident bugles had recalled the Chinese. Wounded
began to fill the warm-up tents where Private Stanley
Robinson lay with tortured feet. Robinson recognized a
buddy among them.

"We get hit?"

"Hit? We got creamed! Everybody's hit. The skipper, Yancey—Kennemore's dead . . ."

Private Robinson struggled to his feet. He pulled on his parka. He grabbed a rifle from among a pile of weapons. He stumbled out into the darkness, ignoring the startled cries of those he left behind him. The cold struck and "shook" him. He moved on, sobbing, his socks sodden from blood and pus issuing from broken blisters. He gained the hill and found Yancey.

Still coughing and spitting, the lieutenant caught sight of the lone reinforcement. He felt his admiration, but had no time to express it. He pointed. "Over there," he shouted hoarsely, "They'll be back—sure as second teeth!"

Robinson hobbled into position, Yancey spat blood into the snow—the cacophony of bugles and whistles rose once more and the Chinese did come back.

They burst the thin dike of Marine resistance. They overran them. Captain Phillips was killed, throwing grenades. Lieutenant Ball died. Wounded lay everywhere. Again Yancey was wounded. A fragment from an exploding grenade tore into his mouth. Still he re-formed a line to counterattack. The battle cry broke from his bloody lips. "Gung ho!" he cried, and they drove forward, Robinson and Gallagher among them. But Yancey fell, struck in the jaw. Though he would live, he could lead no longer. The counterattack failed. Only the wind seemed to lie between the Chinese and North Ridge.

Sergeant Kennemore was alive. He was stretched between blackness and a couch of rock. Battle was raging over him. Cruel feet dug into his body, moving both ways. His ears rang with the pounding of shells, the chatter of guns. Over to his right, he could hear Yancey crying, "Gung ho! Let's go!" And then, "Gung—" There was no more. Yancey must have got it.

Kennemore tried to use his left leg. There was no response. By the light of an exploding shell, by a flare—by the moon even, who would ever know?—by some light he saw his left leg hanging by a shred. He tried his right leg. He could not even gasp his horror as the leg bone came rising up through tattered flesh, like a sword sliding from its sheath.

"My God, my God," he thought. "They're gone. Both of them. I've got to get out of here . . . got to . . ."

He placed his hands beneath him. He shoved. In pain his body moved. He shoved again. He was moving. He was rolling. He rolled down the hillside. He came to rest in the snow. He could not tell where he lay, before or behind his hill. He fumbled for a syrette of morphine. He placed it in his mouth to thaw. He withdrew it and dug it into his flesh. He lay back. And the battle raged around him.

Dawn broke over Kennemore's hill with a cold whiteness that pained the eyeballs. In it, the Marines counterattacked. They drove out and up with swift fury, shooting, clubbing, bayoneting, grenading all before them. They threw the Chinese off the hill.

As they had moved out, some of them passed where Sergeant Kennemore lay. He cried to them weakly. One of them grabbed an empty helmet, scooped it full of snow, handed it to Kennemore, shouted, "Corpsman! Corpsman!" and hurried off to rejoin the attacking line.

Kennemore weakly raised the helmet to his lips and munched the snow. He lay back. His eyes roved dully over the battlefield. He could see Navy corpsmen moving among the bodies, carrying the wounded away on stretchers. He thought: they must be worse than me. He closed his eyes.

There were voices above him, men around him.

"Christ! It's him. It's Kennemore! Hey, you guys with the stretcher. Forget that stiff. This guy's alive!"

The stretcher-bearers stumbled over to Kennemore. Tenderly they rolled him onto the litter. They raised him up. They carried him down the remaining hills to Yudam-ni and the rest of the wounded.

Sergeant Kennemore had made an offering of his life and it was being returned to him—without the legs.

CHAPTER EIGHT

CAPTAIN BARBER's high hill mass would be given the name of Fox Hill, after the company which defended it. But the men of that company, being neither prosaic nor romantic, being given to derision and the sardonic phrase, would think of a dozen better names by ten o'clock on the night of November 27. None of these would be printable, unless an exception may be made for "Cold Ass Heights."

For the place was undoubtedly high, and it was very, very cold.

By ten o'clock Captain Barber and his force of 240 men and officers would be numb in joints and limbs. Their weapons—rifles, BARs, light and heavy machine guns, light and heavy mortars—would be stiff and glassy. Men who could worry in that brainless cold would wonder if their guns would work.

By ten o'clock the men could hear the muted sound of firing to the north. That would keep them awake, especially the men standing the fifty per cent alert on the guns. The other half, in sleeping bags, might be too frozen to care. And the hours would wear on. The sound of battle would rise and fall. That unearthly cold would steadily assert its mastery over human flesh.

By a quarter after one in the morning of the 28th, many of the Marines on watch would be men of stone. Lieutenant Robert McCarthy, hobbling about his lines, would hear no challenges ringing out in that still air. He would seem a solitary stroller on the moon. Angry, McCarthy would assemble his squad leaders and hiss his fury at them.

"Goddam you, keep these men alert!"

Down the order would go, down the immemorial chain of command: "Goddam you, off yer frozen ass!" With kicks and shakes that would not be gentle, the word would be passed along: "Keep alert!"

By two o'clock, McCarthy would pass that way again and hear challenges—angry challenges—and his cracked lips would part in a grin of satisfaction.

At this time, too, Private Hector Cafferata would be satisfied, but for a different reason. There had been a ration issue, it had contained chocolate, and this, by his agreement with Benson, was Cafferata's.

The big man sat upright in his sleeping bag and placed the unyielding disk of chocolate in his mouth. He clenched it between his teeth, half within his mouth, half protruding. He brought the heel of his hand up sharply against the outer half, snapping it in two. His teeth seemed driven into their gums, but he trapped the falling half before it fell to the ground and happily mouthed the other. It would soon melt.

Suddenly Cafferata became aware of the numbness of his feet. He slid his hands down toward them, fumbling for his boots beneath the sleeping bag. He undid them, pushed them off with his feet, and began rubbing his toes. Sharp needles of fire seemed to jab his flesh. But it felt good. He lay back and relaxed. In another hour it would be his and Benson's turn down there in the foxhole where the BAR man and the fire-team leader now stood sentry. He dozed off, wondering if that rumbling sound was gunfire or the nocturnal growling of his buddy's empty belly.

To the right of Cafferata and Benson, Pfc. Gerald Smith and Pfc. Harrison Pomers both led fire teams of riflemen and BARmen. They were awake.

Behind them lay the company's mortars under Lieutenant Joe Brady, Gunnery Sergeant Phillips and manned by such gunners as Pfc. Lloyd O'Leary. They were awake.

Behind them was the Fox Company command post with Captain Barber. He was awake.

And so was an entire regiment of Chinese.

They had surrounded Fox Hill. They had climbed softly through the snow, moving up from The Road where their comrades were already encircling a smaller unit of Marines. Other units were already engaged in building barriers across The Road, dragging logs through the snow, piling them up, mining and booby-trapping them— and then covering them with machine-gun and rifle bunkers dug in on the ridges. Since dark, General Sung's men had been pouring into the hills between Yudam-ni and Hagaru, between Hagaru and Koto-ri, erecting their roadblocks and building up concentrations of fire on the high ground. For General Sung did not believe in closing all avenues of escape to a trapped enemy. It might make him desperate, give him the fury of the cornered rat. No, show him a little daylight—let him burst hopefully from that hole into a helpless net.

So they had been cutting The Road, and now, this regiment of Chinese soldiers was creeping up Fox Hill, massing in a valley before they would go charging up the slopes.

Hector Cafferata snapped awake. That wasn't distant gunfire. That wasn't Ben's belly. That was a *shot!*

The big man squirmed from his sleeping bag, sweeping up his rifle as he jumped to his feet with the yell, "Up, Bens—get yer goddam BAR!"

For the Chinese were coming over the snow. They were dressed in white. They were running at a lope, holding their rifles at high port. Some of them were falling, for the two men out in the foxhole were firing wildly.

"Your boots, Hec!" Benson shouted. "Your boots!"

"Screw the boots!" Cafferata bellowed, and jammed his rifle butt to his shoulder.

The astonished Chinese saw a giant of a man leap suddenly into view with a flaming rifle. Many of them began to fall. They turned their weapons on him, neglecting for a few costly moments those other positions manned by Smith and Pomers. Still exposed, Cafferata fired away—hardly hearing the wild cursing of Benson as he hammered his fists against the steel parts of his frozen, silent BAR.

Cafferata fired unhurriedly—lining them up and squeezing them off, for he was a marksman who was chary with his bullets. The toll was deadly. Perhaps a dozen Chinese perished under that awful accuracy before Cafferata's rifle quit cold on him.

Now neither he nor Benson had weapons.

The first grenades thrown by the oncoming enemy had wounded Lieutenant Brady and Sergeant Phillips. They were out of action. Two other mortarmen were wounded, two others killed. It was up to Pfc. O'Leary to keep the little stovepipes popping at the enemy.

"Up on the hill, O'Leary!" Captain Barber shouted. He had already withdrawn his command post to higher ground, and now he was up on the lines.

O'Leary hastened to obey. Within minutes the men on the lines and Captain Barber heard the welcome sound of Marine mortar shells crunching among the attackers.

But the Chinese were replying with grenades. They fell in showers on the positions of Smith and Pomers. Still their guns continued to chatter and dance, spitting orange flame into the night, with here and there a fat red tracer curving outward on a wide arc. A potato masher fell in Pomers's pit. The men flung themselves on the ground. It went off. No one was hurt. Two more sailed in. These, too, exploded. There were cries of pain. But no one was seriously wounded. A fourth grenade arched over. It landed on Pomers's helmet, exploding at the instant of contact. Pomers sank to the earth.

One of the Marine machine guns fell silent. It had jammed. In an instant a whistle shrilled above the din of battle and a Chinese squad had veered and come charging at the silent position. The gunner swore, yanked his automatic pistol from his holster. He jumped to his feet and fired. He killed six Chinese. The others were cut down by cross fire from Smith's position.

Again a whistle. Again a new direction of Chinese attack. And now it was the trench occupied by Smith's fire team that would receive the full fury of the assault. The Chinese closed, screaming, hurling grenades, and brandishing their bayonets.

Within and around that trench, it was as though some-

one were playing with a light switch—flipping it on and
off—the way the grenades landed and exploded, landed
and roared alight. Everyone in it was dead or wounded
when a big man suddenly jumped inside, to be followed
by a roaring giant, who bellowed: "Gimme a rifle, gimme
a rifle! Mine won't work!"

A wounded Marine shoved a rifle into Cafferata's hands.
"Here," he shouted, "you shoot while I load."

Once more Cafferata stood erect to take the enemy under
fire. He shot off clip after clip, stooping to exchange an
emptied rifle for a freshly loaded one. Smoke curled upward from the barrel-guards, sometimes leaping into
flame. He smothered them with snow and fired on.

A grenade landed on the parapet. Cafferata kicked it
away. Another. Again the kick. A third fell in the trench.
Cafferata seized it and threw—just as it exploded. the
blast tore flesh from his pinkie. A satchel charge sailed in.
Everyone who could move leaped outside. It exploded.
They jumped back in, among the now-dead wounded.

Again a grenade hissed in among them. Benson seized
it and threw. It went off before his eyes. It shattered his
spectacles and temporarily blinded him. He sank down
into the pit, his head roaring, a dull redness veiling his
eyes.

More and more grenades fell, a rain of them. The men
wielded entrenching tools like baseball bats. They struck
at the hissing, grotesquely somersaulting potato mashers
as though they were baseballs, batting them back at the
men who had pitched them. Now the Marines were jumping in and out of the trench like madmen, bayoneting,
clubbing, spreading death and agony, receiving it. Now
the fight for Fox Hill was at its wildest. Dark shapes
flitted and dashed, closed, struggled, fell apart, sank to

the frozen earth, rolled in the snow, staining it with red. Here was the cry, "Marine! Marine!"—and with no answer, the sharp crack of a rifle or the silent thrust of a blade. There were foreign voices raised in challenge—and over all rose the wailing and the keening of the battle, the crunching and crashing of Marine mortars on the slopes, the yellow flashing of the grenades, the muzzle blasts of chattering, barking guns.

The Chinese were falling back. A bugle pealed, gurgled, fell silent. Heavy mortars had joined O'Leary's lights and were pounding the slopes. Marines to either side rolled grenades down the inclines, flushing the enemy into the full fire of Smith's guns. Pfc. Pomers was fighting again, for that ironheaded warrior had regained consciousness and returned to action. Captain Barber was on the lines, directing fire, unscathed and on his feet, though two of his runners had been casualties.

Fox Hill had held.

By daylight only fitful groups of Chinese remained to give battle—sometimes creeping up to the Marine pits to throw their grenades. Individual fights were joined as Marines rushed from their pits to eliminate them. By seven o'clock the Marines were mopping up. Then they were stripping the enemy dead of their guns and bullets, carrying them back to their perimeter. Hector Cafferata was with them, his charred rifle at the ready.

He thought he saw movement among a pile of enemy dead. He approached a Chinese who seemed to breathe. Maybe they could use a prisoner. Half-kneeling, still wary, he peeled back the man's eyeballs. The eyes were raised upward. The man didn't move. Shrugging, Cafferata moved on.

Thud!

Cafferata dived into a snowbank.

Wham!

Shaken, enraged, Cafferata charged back to the "dead" Chinese. "You dirty, rotten bastard," he screamed. Still, no movement. He traced the point of his bayonet on the man's cheek. Not a twitch. He stepped back and shot him in the leg. Not a sign of life. He shot him in the shoulder. The man came up in a sitting position, his eyes open and filled with hate, his lips drawn in a snarl of defiance— treacherous and tough. Cafferata killed him.

He turned and headed back for his lines, and as he did, the war ended for him. An enemy machine gun chattered. Hot flame seared Cafferata's right arm and scorched his armpit. He fell. The bullets whined above him. A Marine started to crawl out to him. Cafferata motioned him back. Using his teeth, he fashioned a bandoleer into a sling for his arm, got half-way back on his feet and lurched to safety.

And that was where he finally collapsed. He had done more than any other man to stem and turn that Chinese flood, and now he could fight no more. In the red fog of his pain, he heard a familiar voice above him.

"Yuh big goon! Ain't yuh got sense enough tuh put yer shoes on?"

It was Sergeant Dee-Jay and he was pointing in astonishment at the big man's feet. They were blue. They were naked. Private Cafferata had fought for five hours, barefoot in the snow.

CHAPTER NINE

WITH the coming of light on the morning of November 28, the 25 miles of road between Koto-ri, Hagaru-ri, and Yudam-ni could be compared to four black beads on a curling white string. The towns and Fox Hill were the beads, and these belonged to General Smith. The Road between was the string, and this was held by General Sung.

He had paid a fearful price for it, had not even succeeded in biting deeply into the lines of the two regiments isolated at Yudam-ni, but The Road was his.

His men had cut it in a dozen places. They held the ridges rising above it. It was dotted with their roadblocks of logs and mines and booby traps. Yudam-ni was entrapped, Fox Hill was surrounded, Hagaru was an island among the enemy and only Koto had friendly road running south to Chinhung and thence to the sea. To the First Marine Division's right, the Army's Task Force Faith was already crumbling under hammer blows of the night before. To their left lay that huge eighty-mile gap.

For all his losses—and they had been fierce—General Sung still held the Marine division in the hollow of his hand. And tonight, when he struck at Hagaru and its airstrip, he would have squeezed them in his fist.

At sunrise on November 28, Colonel Litzenberg and Lieutenant Colonel Murray conferred in the valley of Yudam-ni. Dazed, battered, numbed by the night's events, sorrowing at the loss of friends and the terrible toll among the troops, they fought a sense of shock and an emptiness of spirit. They began to rebuild by forming something rare among professional commanders, men to whom rank and glory mean as much as money and fame to civilians. They set up a council of war.

Though Litzenberg was senior and about to be promoted to brigadier general, he pulled no rank on the youthful, junior Murray, who was also his friend. Their proposal for a council of war was relayed to General Smith in Hagaru, and approved. Henceforth the Fifth and Seventh were combined and directed by joint orders. Henceforth Litzenberg and Murray and their staffs would confer on strategy together.

A flood of orders began to issue from that council. Ground lost during the night was recovered. The ridge where Sergeant Kennemore had been wounded was swept clear of Chinese. How Hill, which might have permitted a breakthrough but for the splendid barrage laid down by the Eleventh Marines, was regained. The perimeter was tightened, reinforced. Service and supply troops and artillerymen were formed into infantry platoons. A thousand wounded were funneled into aid stations and plans were made for helicopter evacuations. The dead were buried. Air support was requested. Even as the regimental commanders conferred, Marine Corsairs were on station in the skies above, swooping on targets singled out for them by the Forward Air Controllers, unloading tanks of Napalm—those horrible fire bombs of jellied gasoline—bombing and strafing the ridges. Down at Fox Hill, Australian pilots in Mustang fighter planes were cheering Captain Barber's men with ridgetop forays.

Slowly, gradually, the activity enforced by those orders began to jolt the Marines from the shock that had inevitably succeeded their wild night of fire. Life, and the will to keep it, came warmly back into numbed bodies now bending to the effort of digging ever deeper into the frozen earth. Korean huts were torn apart for firewood. Working parties were formed to lug ammunition up the hills. The warm-up tents began to empty out.

Soon the Marines were calling encouragement to the "flyboys" who growled in the skies above them, plastering the enemy for them. Groups of Marines danced on the hill crests, shaking their fists and yelling crude jokes at the expense of the married flyers.

"Lookit him, lookit that crazy bastard! He's choppin' wood with his propellers. Yuh kin tell that bastard ain't married!"

They invented bloodcurdling descriptions of Chinese fighting habits for the benefit of those clerks and MP's who appeared among them, their nervous rifle hands and darting eyes betraying their disquiet at having been drafted into the ranks of the foot-sloggers. They laughed at the startled expression on the faces of the tankmen brought from Hagaru by helicopter, after Colonel Litzenberg had found—in that mysterious, inexplicable way of warfare—that there was a new, unscratched, but empty, M-49 tank within his perimeter. "You'll be sorry!" they yelled. "You'll be sorrree!" They fingered the stubble on their chins, balancing cleanliness against the misery of scraping an icy blade over wind-burned flesh, and decided not to shave. They thought it hilarious to hear that the lucky ones such as Pfc. Charles Kaylor had had their stateside journeys broken off at Koto-ri, courtesy of the Communist Chinese. They worried about their weapons, checking them constantly, the machine gunners firing bursts to warm their barrels. They laughed and growled, "Piss on it!" when newly drafted riflemen asked them what to do about a frozen rifle, laughing again to see the childish delight dawning on the faces of those who had the intelligence to follow that coarse but sage advice. They stamped their feet and beat their hands together for warmth, and tried not to notice that there were fewer and fewer airplanes in the skies, that the light was fading— and soon they would be slipping into their frozen holes again, or crawling into sleeping bags, and facing still another night with a prayer for tomorrow.

At Hagaru on that morning of November 28, Major General Oliver P. Smith had been drawing heavily on his second principle of battle: optimism. He sat at a field desk within the Japanese-built bungalow he had chosen for his headquarters. From time to time, he stuck a cold pipe in his mouth and sucked on it reflectively. It was unwise to smoke in that stuffy, evil-smelling shelter. There was smoke enough from the stove, and because they had partitioned the interior with panel dividers, and had taped the windows for warmth, the air was close and foul, reeking with the musty odor of human bodies. Naval Captain Bud Hering, the division's senior medical officer, had pronounced the place a pesthouse and insisted that its oc-

cupants step outside at least once an hour to rid their
lungs of its noxious fumes.

General Smith worked beneath the baleful gaze of a
wall picture of Joseph Stalin. He had left it there, gently
rejecting all suggestions to remove it. "Leave it be," he
had said wryly. "Maybe it'll inspire us."

But it was Smith's optimism that now inspired him.
He did not share the stunned spirit of sleepwalking that
seemed to have filtered down to Tenth Corps from Mac-
Arthur's headquarters. He was only irritated by the war
correspondents' headline talk of "trap" and "approaching
disaster." He saw no trap. True, a look at the map made
it plain that the Eighth Army would have to fall back
farther on the left, leaving that flank of the division un-
guarded. And Task Force Faith on the right was already
in plenty of trouble of its own.

The two regiments at Yudam-ni were alone. But he
could find it fortunate indeed that they had been together
when the Chinese struck. He could be thankful that he
had told Litzenberg to drag his feet on the way up north.
And he could also take comfort in the facts that there
were plenty of supplies in Hagaru, that Partridge's airfield would be ready in three days, and that Puller's regiment had battalions down at Chinhung-ni, at Koto to the
north of that railroad town, and here in Hagaru.

Seeing no trap, Smith acted. He placed the defense of
Hagaru in the hands of Lieutenant Colonel Thomas
Ridge. He got off a message to Litzenberg and Murray,
saying: "Until present situation clarifies, remain present
positions." He arranged for air-drops of supplies to all
the beleaguered points, he remained in contact with Major
General Harris to direct that invaluable close-up air support, he quietly badgered Tenth Corps for a plain order

to meet the situation, and then, so far from fainthearted considerations of what minimum might be salvaged from the Chinese "trap," he began planning for the arrival in Hagaru of Marine replacements and those earlier battle casualties who had been returned to duty. If he was going to continue fighting, he could use more men.

These were among the steps taken by Oliver Smith on the 28th, and far and away the most important was the first: the defense of Hagaru. Even the Korean villagers knew that tonight it would be Hagaru's turn.

All day long, the transports of the Air Force Combat Cargo Command had been flying air-drop missions. They would spot the colored panels set out to identify the Marine lines, and then drop. Parachutes would billow out and the cases of ammunition would come swaying to the earth. Sometimes the pilots missed. The supplies would fall in the no man's land between the Marines and the Chinese. Patrols had to be formed to go out and recover them—under fire and often without weapons, for a rifle hampered a man at such work. The men drew straws. "Well, well," they'd jibe at the glum-faced unfortunate who held the short straw. "If it ain't Lucky Pierre."

It was Lucky Pierre who went.

All day long, the Marine airmen plastered enemy positions. At the one Chinese point overlooking Fox Hill— a rocky promontory from which came sniper fire in daytime, covering fire at night—a plane swooped low and unleashed a tank of Napalm. It came shooting out, almost without describing an arc, bouncing over the rock and then splashing into flame. The Marines cheered. Then, in astonishment, they gaped. The flaming mangled tank was bumping down the hillside. Somehow the Chinese had pushed it over.

"Stupid, ain't they?" Sergeant Dee-Jay growled. "Just a bunch of backward coolies."

At Yudam-ni the last helicopter load of wounded was leaving the perimeter before darkness would fall. Within it were the pilot, one sitting casualty, and a stretcher case. The windows had been knocked out to permit the lower end of the stretcher to be thrust out into the cold. Sergeant Kennemore was on the stretcher. He was terribly cold. Yet he was trying to grin. When he had been examined at the aid station, he had realized that his insides were punctured in many places, that he would lose his legs. But he had been worried about his mangled genitals, dreading the one wound that most men dread. As the doctor had gone over him, he had gazed at him with questioning, agonized eyes. The doctor had shrugged.

"What the hell," the doctor grunted. "Would you worry about half a tank of gas?"

So Kennemore had grinned, and now, as the motor coughed and the blades above him whirled and the helicopter rose into the air, he was hoping that the doctor had not been joking. And the doctor had not been joking, for Sergeant Kennemore would have seven children.

The Road to the south between Koto-ri and Chinhung-ni was still open, and reinforcements were coming up it to Koto. There were three companies of the Army's 185th Engineer Battalion, Company E of the First Medical Battalion, Baker Company of the Army's 31st Infantry Regiment, the 250 men of the Royal British Marines' 41st Commando—jaunty men in battle dress and berets who

had volunteered to serve with their "Yankee cousins"—
George Company of the Third Battalion, First Marines,
and the First Division's Recon Company.

Colonel Chesty Puller welcomed them, personally led
their commanders into positions, and then ascended a
ridge with an aide to sweep the surrounding hillsides with
field glasses. To his front he could see Chinese. To the left
and right he could see them. Even to his rear there were
Chinese moving along the hills preparatory to cutting
Koto off from Chinhung-ni. Puller put down the glasses
and turned to his aide. "They've got us surrounded," he
rasped. Then, grinning through lips cracked and blue with
cold, he added: "The bastards won't get away this time!"

Up at Hagaru Lieutenant Colonel Ridge was not so
cocky. He was puzzled. Like Litzenberg, he had been provided with intelligence outlining the enemy's plan of battle
for the night. Ridge's information had come from a dozen
South Korean "line-crossers" whom he had screened and
trained in the early days before The Road. They were
under his intelligence officer, Second Lieutenant Richard
Carey.

Carey had been sending them into the hills for the past
twenty four hours, and they had been returning with a
single, unvarying report: "A division of Chinese has
moved south from the Reservoir and will attack Hagaru
at 9:30 o'clock on the night of the 28th."

Could he believe it? Well, events had proved Litzenberg's coolie soldiers to be dead right. Ridge decided to
believe his Koreans. Having settled that, he now had to
consider his forces, and these would not seem to inspire
cockiness in any battalion commander facing a division
of enemy. Of Marine rifle companies he had only Item and

How of his own Third Battalion, First. After that, he had a motley of cooks, bakers, signalmen, MP's, drivers, clerks, and sundry other service people. The great majority were Marines, though there were also Army engineer, signal, and service units from Tenth Corps. It was a ragtag-bobtail, but Ridge began to put it into line.

Expecting the Chinese to attack from the south, that is, to the left facing uproad and below the airfield, he put his rifle companies in line there. These were his strongest. Above the town and the airfield, he put his Marine service troops. In the hills to the east, or right, of Hagaru, he put the three Army units under a Marine officer, Captain John Shelnutt.

He put them in line, into a potato-shaped perimeter encompassing both town and airfield, and told them to dig in.

Dig in?

Lieutenant Joe Fisher's Item Company had been doing hardly anything else since they had taken over their position from Fox Company, Seventh, the day before. The Bull had deduced that any enemy attack against Hagaru might come in strength against him. He had set his men to work "borrowing" C-3 explosive from the engineers. This was shaped in empty ration cans. A hole was bored in the rocklike ground. The shaped charge was placed inside. A sandbag went over it and everyone took off.

Ba-loom!

When the men returned, they scooped the loose dirt from beneath the split surface, shoveled it into sandbags which had also been "borrowed," and built their fortifications. Extra shaped charges were placed out in front as improvised land mines.

There were strands of barbed wire strung on logs. In front of them, along the corridor the Chinese would have to use, Fisher's men wove a deadly maze of trip flares, mines, and booby traps. Grenades were taped to stakes and stumps, their loosened pins connected to ankle-level trip wires. Five-gallon cans of gasoline, with thermite grenades similarly "fixed," were placed at strategic points to light the battle. Two of the larger native houses were singled out for tracer fire, and more illumination, upon an order from Fisher.

Before dark Fisher made his final inspection. He made sure that each warm-up tent had been stocked with a five-gallon can of hot coffee. He eyed the piles of grenades and bandoleers and belts of small-arms ammunition in the trenches and was satisfied. He came up to a rifleman's hole and kicked with his foot against the inbound side.

"Just so you'll know, your alternative position is—"

"Sir?" the rifleman interrupted, astonished. "My alternative *what?*"

"—is right here," Fisher finished, grinning. "Right on the other side of this hole!"

Then he returned to his command post, while darkness fell on the little Korean hill town, looking so much now like a mining camp transplanted from the Klondike—its tents, its rough buildings, its bare frozen earth, and around it all, the bleak snowy mass of the mountains.

Up at Yudam-ni, Colonel Litzenberg had had to make a tough decision. Most of his regiment's Cook Company had been encircled the night before, at a point on The Road above Fox Hill. He had to get them back. But in sending Lieutenant Colonel Raymond C. Davis down for them with his First Battalion, Seventh, he was taking a chance. Davis's sector held a hill guarding the avenue into Yudam-ni. The Chinese might choose to try it at any time. But he held his breath, sent Davis and his men south, and plugged the gap with "irregulars" from service, headquarters, and artillery units.

Not until Cook Company and the First Battalion came back, coming in three hours after dark and carrying their casualties from the fight that broke the Chinese hold, did Blitzin' Litzen breathe easily. Even though the "irregulars" had to stay on the hill, Litzenberg now had a good-sized reserve in the perimeter, and he and Murray were ready.

They were ready at Fox Hill, too.

Captain Barber had been assured of artillery support from Hagaru, and the air-drop had brought illumination shells for the light mortars. He was sure he could hold. He had said that to Yudam-ni, when orders had come to break out of Fox Hill and go to the relief of Cook Company. He had said he didn't think he could make it, but that he could hold where he was. He hadn't said why he didn't want to depart Fox Hill: that he couldn't take his wounded, and he wasn't going to leave them.

Pfc. Ken Benson was also pleased. He was proud of the device he had rigged for the Chinese. In the afternoon, as his sight cleared and he could think of other things, he had realized that he had lost his gloves. He had slipped down the slope to the spot where he and Cafferata had slept the night before. He had found their sleeping bags in tattered hanks and puffs of feathers. The Chinese had shot them up, thinking there were sleepers in them, and then sliced them with bayonets. Coming back, he approached the grizzled Sergeant Dee-Jay.

"Listen," he said. "Why don't we take the dead guys' sleeping bags and plant them out there? Put them in kind've a ring. Maybe the Chinks will stop to shoot them up, and we can sight in on them."

"Good idea," the sergeant grunted, and they had taken the bags, stuffed them with snow, and set them thirty yards down the slope.

Like the skipper, they were ready.

CHAPTER TEN

ISOLATE them. Separate them from one another. Cut their line of supply and seize their strong points. Then destroy them piecemeal.

This, in sum, had been the battle plan of General Sung Shin-lun. It remained so on the second night, guiding the fourfold movement begun with the dark and the coming of snow.

He would hit and hold them at Yudam-ni.

He would obliterate them at Fox Hill.

He would overwhelm them at Hagaru-ri.

He would draw a bristling line of men and guns and roadblocks between Koto-ri and Chinhung-ni.

Elsewhere, wherever possible along The Road, bridges would be blown and roadblocks reinforced.

On this second night, with the snow to conceal the massing of his men and to deny the air to night-flying American planes, General Sung would close his fist.

They came again at Yudam-ni. They attacked from the north in numbers far, far less than on the preceding night. For the first time they opened up with artillery—

76mm rifles. But the 105's of the Eleventh Marines bayed back at them with swift, eager voices and the Chinese guns fell silent.

Yudam-ni had a quiet night.

But Fox Hill was again inflamed. In the hush of a snowy darkness, Captain Barber's men had been able to hear them gathering below. Chattering to each other, blowing whistles, clanging cymbals, they massed with a careless clatter that made a fiction of that celebrated Oriental stealth.

To Captain Barber it was obvious that the assault would once more come up the western slope. To the men crouched in holes often barricaded with frozen enemy bodies, this also became obvious—once the rocky ridge above came alive with automatic weapons laying down a covering fire.

Once again the bugle calls, again the squat white figures pelting up the slope, again the sudden clamor of battle.

But now Pfc. O'Leary's mortars were dropping illumination shells among them. The snowflakes seemed to glisten in that sharp white light. In it, against the backdrop of the night beyond, the Chinese were caught and framed as though on stage. A crackling fire swept through them. Heavy mortars and now the shells of the artillery crashed among their reserves, filling the air with flying bits of steel and flesh and rock. Snowbanks leaped skyward, dissolving in glittering plumes of misty white—like waves breaking on rock.

Even without his glasses Pfc. Benson could see the enemy plainly. He saw a squad coming at a lope—then pause at his circle of "sleeping men." They lowered their weapons and pumped bullets into them. Men with bayonets

swung their blades. Benson and his sergeant and the other
Marines around them carefully sighted in on this clump
of stamping, whirling, berserk enemy and cut them down.

Captain Barber was almost on the line of battle, calling
his encouragement, directing fire. He slumped to the
ground. Enemy bullets had pierced his left leg on the
outer side below the knee, passing through and continuing
on out the other leg. He pulled himself painfully to a
sitting position. He called for a Marine to support him,
and struggled erect, and stayed to fight.

The wounded were restless. Those corpsmen who could
be spared from the lines were going softly among them,
cupping candles with their hands. Everyone conscious
could hear the battle, could cringe at the sound of the
bullets pinging sharply through the tent canvas. Hector
Cafferata felt ashamed. He should be out there with Bens.
He pulled himself up and groaned. A corpsman scurried
over.

"Lay down," the corpsman hissed.

"But I should be out there," Cafferata muttered. He
groaned again. There was something hurting him in the
chest.

Holding his guttering light, the corpsman stooped,
opened Cafferata's garments, and peered at his chest.
Below the breastbone was a tiny red hole.

"You damn fool!" he hissed again. "Lay down!"

"I ain't that bad."

"If it'll make you feel better, you couldn't be worse!"

Cafferata sank back into the darkness. He was no longer
ashamed.

Pain had also stabbed at Captain Barber again, but
he couldn't be sure of where he had been hit. More important to him, he was winning. The Chinese were not

penetrating as far as they had come the previous night. The flares, the artillery, and the practice of his men were keeping them off. Only one of his automatic weapons seemed to be silenced. In the morning he would find that pit, the mounds of bodies before it so high that it had lost its field of fire. And the hole would be empty. The two men who had held it would never be found.

Out perhaps twenty yards to the front, leftward, stood a Chinese bugler, fixed in the light of a falling flare. He pressed his horn to his lips. He was motionless, a heroic figure out of an antiquity when Mongol ponies trod the earth of Europe and yak-tails swung at the tents of the Golden Camp. He began to blow.

"Lemme fix that bastard!" a Marine cried hoarsely, and a grenade sped in a swift flat arc toward the bugler.

It landed almost at his feet. The bugle still blared, and there was a flash and a roar, intermixed with the long, trailing wail of a horn—and the din of battle reclaimed all ears.

Now the Marines were blowing captured whistles, confusing the attackers. Now some of the Chinese seemed to be veering off into the dark—swift as the snowflakes passing through fields of light—as though terrified to come up that fiery slope. Now it was plain that Fox Hill was going to hold, although morning would show that of the 240 men who had begun its defense, less than half of them would be able to fight on.

It was half past nine on the same night at Hagaru. And the Chinese had not shown up on schedule. But nerves drawn taut since the beginning of the 100 per cent alert continued to twang like plucked wire. Men began to mutter uneasily on the airfield line held by Fisher's Item

Company and Captain Clarence Corley's How Company.

"The Goo-Goos are late."

"Yeah, mebbe they're on daylight saving."

"Or they lost their way."

"Lost? Even a shavetail couldn't get lost with that god-dam airfield back there lighted up like a Christmas tree!"

"You know it, boy. Only the Jarheads'd be stupid enough to fight under floodlights!"

There was more of it, until the voices of authority hissed sharply out of the black. "Knock it off, there! Shaddap and keep alert!"

So they peered anxiously into the falling snow, while behind them, under a flood of electric light, the engineers rode their graders and scrapers, sometimes pausing with a bitter curse to seize a jackhammer and free the blades of clumps of frozen earth. And then, at half past ten, the Chinese showed up.

Three red flares, three whistle blasts—and suddenly they were there.

They seemed to pop up out of the snow.

"They're here!" a How Company gunner yelled. "They must've rolled down the slopes."

They had. And as they launched their charge, the grenadiers in front hurling their hissing potato mashers, the Marine lines were pounded savagely by mortar and white phosphorous shells. The bombardments had dreadful effect. How Company was being steadily whittled. Its ranks were thinning, and the Chinese began a skillful exploitation of their supporting fire. They came charging in neat waves, following up each bombardment. There was no concerted rush of a yelling horde. Even in the snow-streaming dark, the Chinese seemed to know their objectives. Spraying with burp guns, tossing grenades, the light machine-gunners charging and firing as they charged, they swerved and redeployed upon a whistle blast. Even though staggered by an awful Marine cross fire, which seemed to spread a network of flashing tracers above the ground, they struck and restruck at How Company. And Captain Corley found himself in the dark, his communications out, his wire to battalion cut, one of his platoon leaders already dead in the center, his right platoon heavily engaged, and the Chinese mounting still more furious assaults. He radioed to battalion for reinforcements, then joined a fire team laying down a covering fire while First Lieutenant Harrison Betts took a counterattack up against the point where How Company's line was bending.

But Betts and a fresh Chinese force met head-on, and the Marines were beaten to the ground.

Now the Chinese had an opening. Men poured into the gap, stumbling over the writhing bodies of comrades cut down by fire still coming from the Marine flanks, and burst through.

And then, having fought so furiously to obtain that penetration, they threw it away. Valor, skill, high resolve had brought them through Marine steel, and then they seemed to sink in a swamp of their own stupidity. They milled around, even though they had the command post and the galley surrounded. They went off on a looting spree. They tore through the galley stores like pack rats. They scrambled for clothing and fought each other for it. They shot up sleeping bags and slashed aimlessly at warming tents, not pausing to look inside, and they hacked at stores they could not carry off. One wounded Marine saved his life by lying limp while two Chinese tore his parka from him.

The Chinese had become despoilers, driven by a mindless energy that carried one group as far as the airfield.

And if ever East met West with the shock of astonishment felt on both sides, it was at that moment when the snow-capped foot soldiers of Sung Shin-lun burst from the dark into the glare of electric bulbs that lighted the work of those busily scraping and gouging engineers. There were wild shouts in tongues that neither side understood, the clanging of bullets off the steel sides of the tractors—and then the engineers leaped to the ground, unslung their rifles, and routed the Chinese in a counterattack led by Second Lieutenant Robert McFarland. Whereupon those doughty shakers and movers of earth reslung their weapons and went back to work, victors in Korea's first battle fought under the floodlights.

But there was still that gap in How Company's lines, and Ridge, realizing the desperation of the situation, quickly sent fifty Army and Marine service people up to the front under First Lieutenant Grady Mitchell. Almost immediately Mitchell was killed. The men faltered. First Lieutenant Horace Johnson ran to them in the dark, rounded them up, and redeployed them in a ditch. Another counterattack was mounted, with Lieutenant Betts and Tech Sergeant Robert Barnes leading a group of thirty Marines. White phosphorous shells exploded among them with terrible effect. Marines fell everywhere.

"Follow me!" Betts screamed, dashing toward the bulk of an empty house suddenly framed in the light of an exploding shell. If they could reach it, they would have driven a wedge into the gap. The Marines followed. Two more phosphorous shells splashed among them. Only eight men and Betts remained standing. But they made the hut, with all but Betts wounded, and they held it throughout the night, until the morning's counterattack relieved them and erased the bulge.

Within the potato of that perimeter, no man moved except at a crouch, for bullets and fragments of steel sped everywhere above the ground. Even the walls of division headquarters were pierced and torn.

General Smith worked on at his desk, and then a hail of bullets struck the kitchen. They hit the stove and ricocheted wildly around the room, raising a witch's clatter among the pots and pans.

"Are you all right?" General Smith called to the mess sergeant in the kitchen, and the blistering reply that rushed back at him gave profane assurance that although there may not be much left to cook with, General Smith still had a cook.

Item Company was holding. Bull Fisher and his men were holding as perhaps no line had ever held before.

The Chinese blundered into that wicked labyrinth of trip flares, booby traps, land mines, and cans of gasoline— all covered by machine guns, rifles, and mortars—and they met annihilation there. Only three Chinese came within closing distance of a Marine. They rushed at Second Lieutenant Wayne Hall, certain of their man when they saw he could not fire his carbine. But Hall drew his pistol and killed all three, the last pitching forward into his hole.

Otherwise the carnage was incredible.

Roaming the lines, his great figure a splendid target, Fisher called down 1,700 mortar shells upon those crumpling, trapped Chinese. At midnight the tracers of his machine guns fingered the Korean huts with fire and set them blazing. And then the carnage was complete.

That was how Item Company held, with two men killed and sixteen wounded. And when dawn crept sullenly over that frozen southern battlefield, souvenir hunters who picked their wary way among the red-stained, snow-covered mounds that once were living men counted up to 750 of them, before the arrival of Marine air sent them scurrying back to their pits.

East Hill had been overrun.

Ridge's worst fears had been realized. Throughout the afternoon of the 28th, he had hoped that his George Company would be able to force its way up The Road from Koto-ri. But they had been halted at a roadblock, turned back. Now Ridge was forced to cover East Hill—that is, the right-hand curve of his perimeter—with Captain Shelnutt's untrained force of about two hundred Army engineers from Tenth Corps. And of these perhaps half were green South Korean troops, who spoke no English. These were the ROK's of the "buddy system" forced upon under-strength Army units. They were assigned to American "buddies" in the vain hope that they would learn quickly, perhaps pick up a little English.

This was the ragged force that made the exhausting climb of East Hill in the late hours of day. Slipping and sliding over ice and frozen rocks, carrying stores of ammunition, they pulled themselves up the steep face of that six-hundred-foot-high hill. When they got there, some were lucky enough to occupy positions already dug. Most of them had no cover. Many had frozen weapons. Some of the ROKs didn't know how to use them. But by dark Captain Shelnutt reported through his radio operator, Pfc. Bruno Podolak, that they were in position.

Lieutenant-Colonel Ridge's relief quickly gave way to

a prayer that the Chinese would not strike East Hill. By two o'clock in the morning of the 29th, he knew that his prayer had been answered, and that the answer was "No!"

"Under heavy attack," Shelnutt radioed.

Thirty minutes later Shelnutt was dead and Pfc. Podolak was the only living American on East Hill.

The Communists had hit with shattering force. They had obliterated a ROK platoon on the left, many of whom perished without firing a shot, and rolled up the flank of Shelnutt's engineers in a fury that threw them all the way down the hill.

"I'm alone up here," Podolak reported, his voice sunk to a whisper. "I can't get down with this heavy gear. I'll hide somewhere and keep you informed."

Podolak kept his promise. He kept Ridge supplied with a steady flow of situation reports, all of which were bleak. In sum, Podolak reported that the Chinese held East Hill in battalion strength and they were digging in.

Ridge called for artillery. He ordered a counterattack. While How Battery of the Eleventh Marines shifted trails, reversed guns, and drew a curtain of steel across the gap, pounding the Chinese massing areas in the ravines and lowlands beyond, Ridge's executive officer, Major Reginald Myers, hastened to collect all available Marines and to rally East Hill's routed defenders for a counterthrust.

For East Hill could not be lost. It aimed a dagger at the throat of Hagaru. It threatened the Marine lines to either side. All this was clear to Myers as he led his reserve of Marines to the roadside ditch where he found most of the engineers. They were huddled together, cold, stunned, demoralized. Myers moved among them, urging, commanding, organizing. The dull light of dawn was be-

hind the hill before he had at last re-formed a skirmish
line and started upward.

How Battery lifted fire. Its 105's had sent 1,200 rounds
howling into the black, and now it was time to knock it
off and let the tanks and mortars take over. They blasted
the hilltop. Myers began his attack.

Unfeeling lumps for feet . . . ice and glassy rocks for
handholds . . . sobbing breath and tortured lungs . . .
sweating and freezing in your own sweat . . . dodging
grenades rolling downhill . . . clattering fall and broken
bones . . . And always the enemy machine gunners raking
your ranks. Sometimes they would falter, crawl for cover,
slip off into the holes and crevices of that cut-up hill mass.
Myers would move among them in a rage of command.
He would shove them, shout at them, drive them ever upward. And as steadily as the line advanced, so steadily did
it dwindle.

At last Myers had drawn a thin line below the crest of
the hill. He had been joined by Podolak and radioed back
that he had 75 men—60 Marines and 15 soldiers—of the
300 who had begun the climb. He could not take the hill,
even though Marine air was now working over the enemy's
positions, but he could hold that line.

They began to fight to hold it. Podolak was shot in the
back, but the heavy radio that had held him at his post
now saved his life; merely wounded, he fought on.

Ridge rushed reinforcements around the other side of
East Hill. But this irregular force, under Lieutenant Nick
Canzona, was also unable to dislodge the Chinese.

The day would wear on, and Myers would still hold.
But for so long as the Marines remained in Hagaru, only
that narrow line and the guns of the artillery would contain the Chinese who now commanded East Hill.

CHAPTER ELEVEN

It was the third day of ordeal—November 29—and to Major General Oliver P. Smith it marked the end of the beginning.

Hagaru had held, and tomorrow the airport would be ready. Though East Hill remained a trouble spot, Ridge and the artillery could handle it at least until nightfall.

Yudam-ni was secure and Fox Hill was hanging on, even if only by the eyelashes.

Koto had had a visit from the enemy, but Puller had beaten them back. Chinhung-ni was still in Marine hands, though cut off now from Koto. But an Army task force was coming up from Hamhung to reinforce it.

In the mind of Oliver Smith, a chain of place names had begun forming in a string. Yudam-ni . . . Fox Hill . . . Hagaru-ri . . . Koto-ri . . . Chinhung-ni . . . Hamhung and The Road to the sea. Break out of Yudam to Fox Hill in an eight-mile thrust. Drive the remaining six miles to Hagaru. Regroup and break out to Koto along another eleven miles. Re-form again and punch ten more miles to Chinhung—and the last forty-three miles would be comparatively easy. Why not? Xenophon had done it. And as Louie Puller would say, Xenophon wasn't even leading Marines.

That would be the plan, presented to Oliver Smith by the situation—as had happened to Xenophon. Like that immortal Greek, Smith must conduct a fighting march through the ranks of a numerous encircling Oriental foe, must move along a treacherous mountain road by seizing the high ground above the passes, and must at last debouch in safety on the sea. Though Smith's Americans and handful of Britishers and South Koreans had but 78 miles to go, in comparison to the 1,500 miles covered by Xenophon's Greeks, they must move quickly, in bitter cold, in blizzards, in a barren land yielding no food or sanctuary. They must fight toward each other, against modern arms that would multiply the miles and against a trained enemy led by a skillful commander with a careful plan of annihilation. In balance, the odds were the same. And they would get out, too. The arms of the modern West would have a new Anabasis.

Thus the plan was forming. But having reviewed the best aspects of the ordeal, General Smith now turned to the worst ones.

First, the night's fighting at Hagaru had been costly. The number of dead was not known, though it was probably about 200, and there were already 500 casualties in the town's hospital tents. More were being brought down from the fighting continuing atop East Hill. Hagaru needed reinforcements badly, especially trained and seasoned line troops to stiffen Ridge's bobtail battalion and to reinforce Myers on East Hill. General Smith telephoned Colonel Puller in Koto-ri and ordered him to send all the men he could spare up The Road to Hagaru.

Second, the Fifth and Seventh Regiments at Yudam-ni

must reverse their positions preparatory to their breakout. An attack to the Yalu was now out of the question.
The east-west line of fortified hills which the Fifth and
Seventh held to mount that assault must now be shifted
to a north-south alignment. Relative to The Road, they
would have to move from a left-to-right line into a fore-
and-aft position. Smith contacted Tenth Corps with this
proposal, received permission to execute it, and sent the
order north.

Third, there were his flanks. No use to worry about the
left. It was gone. The Eighth Army was still retreating.
The right? He conferred with Major General David G.
Barr, who had flown in a helicopter up to the right side
of the Reservoir where Task Force Faith was engaged.
Barr told him that Lieutenant Colonel Faith was preparing a fighting breakout to Hagaru. Good. He could
use those men when they arrived.

So General Smith was ready. Another night, one more
day, and this white-maned optimist in battle would order
his First Marine Division to come out fighting.

General Sung Shin-lun had a few fighting orders left
himself, but his optimism was on the ebb. His casualties
were atrocious. To read them filled him with bitter rage
and sorrow. He groaned at the recollection of his artillery,
left across the Yalu. Without it, with but a scattering of
heavy guns, with only mortars to soften the Marine positions, his division commanders had been forced to send
their soldiers charging into terrible concentrations of fire.
Worse, some of his units had already expended their ammunition. Chinese soldiers carry three days' fire, and many
of them had been in battle for three days. They had no
bullets left.

The American air attacks were mounting. By day they broke up troop assemblies, interdicted the open spaces, roared low with flaming guns to support Marine counter-attacks. And now they were beginning to rake those farm-houses and village huts which had provided the chief shelter and concealment for his men. They were appearing at night, too.

General Sung did not like to think of his wounded. He had seen them staggering north, dragging themselves through the snow, trailing a ragged wake of red behind them. There was little medical help for them. A casualty who could not fight again was ordered to take himself home, over the hills and across the Yalu. And many of them died of wounds en route, if they did not first freeze to death.

That winter which had made a cold white glittering hell of all those hills was also stiffening and loosening the fist in which General Sung had thought he held the American Marines. Frostbite had already thinned his forces as much as enemy fire. Those pitiful sneakers his men wore, little enough protection against the biting frost, were often slashed to tatters by the cruel rocks. Those quilted coats of cotton were frozen as stiff as armor. And the cotton gloves! General Sung had heard reports of men whose hands had frozen to their weapons, whose fingers had to be broken free. That ration of powdered grain had stiffened into hard cakes, inedible.

Though ruthless, though a battle-hardened Communist possessed of that Oriental contempt for the lives of others, General Sung knew men. He knew the limits of human endurance, and beneath his furies ran a cold understanding of why his starving, freezing soldiers had acted like stupid ravening wolves during those miserably few occasions on which they had burst the enemy's lines.

Knowing this, feeling the fingers of the trap turn brittle, he realized that only quick action could save his plan. He must try a third time. Fox Hill must be down to a helpless remnant, for the Americans were also made of flesh.

Fox Hill would fall. Hagaru must have been whittled, and it could not be reinforced.

But General Sung Shin-lun was wrong on both counts, Reinforcements were already forcing The Road to Hagaru from Koto-ri, and Fox Hill still had plenty of fight.

There were boards tied to Captain William Barber's legs. They helped him stand erect, and with a Marine to lend him his shoulder, he could still hobble around the lines.

"How's it going, Smith?"

"Fine, sir. The eggs this morning were wonderful, and I hear there's steak tonight."

"You know it, boy—and plenty of baked Alaska for desert."

"Benson! What in hell have you got there?"

"A Nambu, sir. A Jap machine gun. I took it off a Chink. And damned if it doesn't fire wooden bullets!"

"Well, so long as it fires. Stay loose, boy."

"God almighty damn, Sergeant! Are your men having a masquerade?"

"No, sir! Them things they got on is parachutes. We got 'em from the air drops. They may look like kimonos, sir, but they're warm as hell!"

"Good. Send a few up to the wounded, will you? They can use them."

And the wounded are uneasy.
Lying in the dimly lighted tent, they have had time to think. They can wonder if the company will have to fight its way out. They know they can't walk. What will happen to them? Captain Barber can sense their disquiet at the painful moment he stoops to enter their tent.
"All right, men, here it is. Things are pretty bad. But I've seen them worse. And—one thing—we're not pulling off this hill unless we all go together. And nobody stays unless we all stay together. That's it."
A long silence follows the captain's departure, and then, slowly, self-consciously, the wounded begin to talk again.

Task Force Drysdale was leaving Koto-ri.
Some 900 men, some 150 vehicles, some 30 tanks—a long, winding, bristling column of men and arms was coming to the relief of Hagaru. But it was also moving into ambush.
Colonel Puller had christened the column Task Force Drysdale after its commander, Lieutenant Colonel Douglas Drysdale of the British Royal Marines' 41st Commando. It was Drysdale's men, still jaunty in berets, still contemptuous of helmets, who were leading the assault.
They had had an inspection before they jumped off. They had stood in ranks, ramrod-straight, their weapons slung, while their officers moved among them—and around them snipers' bullets sighed for flesh or spanged off frozen earth.
Seeing them, their Yankee cousins, those sardonic slog-

gers who call themselves "the raggedy-assed Marines" and who care more for spit than for polish, these bearded and baggy Jarheads were merely astonished.

"Gawd a'mighty damn, if they ain't everyone of 'em shaved!"

"Aw, them limeys is always on stage, puttin' on a show."

"Mebbe so, but it's a damn good show!"

It was, and at a command, weapons still slung, the Royal Marines moved out in the point, fighting with American Marines for the first time since the Boxer Rebellion a half century before. In their trace moved George Company of the Third Battalion, First, commanded by Captain Carl Sitter. These two units would alternate in leading the fighting advance—41st Commando to seize the first enemy position, George Company to move through them and on to the next, and so to leapfrog up The Road.

Following them was Baker Company of the Army's 31st Regiment. Bunched in the center was another of those hodgepodges that had become so common since November 27—Marine service troops, MP's, truck drivers, signalmen, headquarters clerks.

A motor column under Major Henry Seeley brought up the rear, and there were tanks at either end of the entire task force.

To either side of the nine miles of road before them were two divisions of Chinese. They were well entrenched. They were fifteen or sixteen thousand men against less than a thousand. But the tanks clanked forward and the British Marines marched out, even as Marine artillery and mortars rained a heavy fire on the first enemy height about a half mile above the northern rim of Koto's perim-

eter. Air support had been scheduled, too, but it hadn't
shown up. Drysdale approached Major Whitman Bartley,
the Supporting Arms Co-ordinator.

"Where's the air?"

"Colonel, only an act of God will get it here on time.
It's all going up to Yudam-ni."

Drysdale looked at his watch.

"I'll give you five minutes."

He strode away.

My God, Bartley thought, they *do* act like that. Just
like it says in Kipling. Then, above him, he heard the
motors of two Marine Corsairs, proof enough that there
was a kind of magic in that sort of thing. Frantically he
contacted the Forward Air Controller, who got in touch
with the Corsairs, directed them to their targets, and
brought tanks of Napalm, bombs, and bullets down upon
the Chinese.

In exactly five minutes.

Lieutenant Colonel Drysdale was evidently pleased, and
he ordered his 41st Commando up the hill. They went up
in parade-ground formation, weapons still slung, walking
four or five paces apart. Mortars fell among them and
dropped on their comrades gathering at the roadside to
support them. They took heavy casualties, but they continued on to drive the Chinese from the first knoll. Then
George Company passed through them to seize the next
hill, about a mile and a half north of Koto and to the
right of the advance. The American Marines met heavy
small-arms fire from hillside bunkers. They placed a 3.5
rocket launcher into action. It reduced the bunkers and
the hill was taken. Forty-first Commando leapfrogged
ahead, and the first enemy barrier had fallen.

Now the tail of Task Force Drysdale dragged slowly out of Koto-ri. But at half past eleven the entire column halted.

At another hill farther up The Road, and also to the right, both Marine companies had run into fierce resistance. Chinese machine-gun fire was supported by heavy mortars. The Marines were stopped.

Drysdale brought both companies down to The Road and waited there for further orders from Koto. He was informed that eight more tanks were clanking north to reinforce him. But they would not arrive until late afternoon. Drysdale began re-forming his column to punch still farther north, past that unconquerable Chinese hill.

But the narrowness of The Road, the difficulty of maneuvering vehicles into line again beneath constant enemy fire, delayed him until about two o'clock in the afternoon. Then, with the Marines of George Company leading, 41st Commando following, and the Army's Baker Company in third position, the fighting head of Task Force Drysdale lurched uproad again.

These three units received punishing fire. One Chinese mortar landed in a George Company truck and wounded every man aboard. Chinese riflemen and light machine gunners barricaded themselves in roadside huts to pour a steady fire into the Americans and British. Each time one of Drysdale's tanks deployed to blast a Chinese strong point or to skirt a crater in The Road, the assault troops had to leap from their trucks and scramble for roadside ditches. Each time such obstacles were overcome, the troops had to remount their vehicles. It was a toiling, inching progress—stop and fight, start and stop to fight again. It was a joint-by-joint advance, like a caterpillar's—the point in movement, the middle slowing, the rear halted, and then the ripple of movement commencing at the rear and slowing to immobility at the point. And gaps were widening between the British and American Marines in the van and Baker Company—and between Baker Company and all those following units of Task Force Drysdale.

All the while, heavy small-arms fire was raking them. Bullets were pinging and spanging, men were being hit and crying out in pain or slumping into death. The wounded needed help. Trucks would jolt to a halt, the cry of "Corpsman!" would be raised, and whatever lay behind must halt until the wounded man had been given aid.

Though Marine fighters on station in the skies above —usually two, never more than four—harried the enemy incessantly, they were scarcely denting his forces. Air reports of hillsides "crawling with Chinese" were mounting steadily. There was no need to search for targets, they abounded. There were too many targets and not enough planes.

About four miles north of Koto, the column stopped again. The time was a quarter past four. At that very minute, Drysdale's tank reinforcements were rumbling out of Koto-ri.

But Drysdale was not concerned about them. He was alarmed by a report brought back by two of his own tanks which had sortied a half mile above him. The tankmen said the path ahead was impassable. There were too many Chinese. On the right-hand ridges alone, three battalions were dug in. Tanks and supporting infantrymen might make it to Hagaru, but the trucks wouldn't.

If Drysdale pressed on, he advanced into ambush.

The task force commander sent a message to General Smith in Hagaru, telling him that the vehicular train could not get through, but that he could fight his way on foot if so ordered. Back came General Smith's reply:

"Come ahead at all costs."

Drysdale shrugged. His retort was as clipped as his accent. "Very well, we'll give them a show," he said, and ordered his column north again.

Now there was further delay while the tanks refueled. Now the shadows were lengthening in the valleys. Now it was dark, and the tanks, American Marines, and 41st Commando were fighting forward again, leaving behind them their stalled trucks and jeeps, most of Baker Company, and that hodge-podge of headquarters and service troops in their own vehicles, plus the rear guard and reinforcement of tanks, which had joined forces. Now the attacking column's radio was shot out and there was neither communication nor control—and now, halfway to Hagaru, as George Company approached a narrow defile winding beneath a steep bluff to the right, the men of General Sung Shin-lun pulled the string.

The hillsides roared and flashed with light. Hundreds of little red eyes winked on the slopes. Mortars crashed among the trucks and scrambling men with a steadiness that seemed to permit no interval of silence between explosions.

Captain Sitter's men were bearing the brunt of it, taking to the ditches while the Marine tanks swerved and roared in answering fire. Sitter's jeep was knocked out. Two of his officers were wounded. Drysdale was hit. His assistant was hit. British and American Marines were falling. A withering fire swept into the ranks of the soldiers in Baker Company. But George Company and 41st Commando still punched northward through that hellish fire.

The Chinese were coming down, closing to grenade-throwing range. A hissing object fell with a clatter into a truck crowded with Marines.

"Grenade!"

Pfc. William Baugh threw himself on it, smothering the explosion with his body. He died so that all his comrades might live.

In and out of the trucks, fight on, follow the tanks, force a passage.

The tanks clattered into Hagaru. Sitter's George Company staggered in after them. Forty-first Commando was still fighting, forcing the defile. To their rear an ammunition truck blew up. They fought on in the light of its flames, bursting roadblock after roadblock. Units were cut off, surrounded—and they blasted their way out. Almost all of the unit's officers were dead or wounded. But 41st Commando got through. At half past one in the morning of November 30, sixteen and a half hours after departing Koto, Drysdale's Royal Marine were within the perimeter of Hagaru-ri. He had come on "at all costs," and the costs had been high. He had lost half of his 41st Commando.

And behind him, in that low-lying halfway point that would be called Hell-Fire Valley, the remaining men and vehicles of Task Force Drysdale had been trapped and sliced into four sections, just as they attempted to turn their trucks around for a fighting return to Koto.

Fox Hill was on fire again.

The Chinese were there again, the same time, the same place. Again the whistles, bugles, cymbals; again the Marine artillery, the mortar flares, the defenders crouching in their holes, colder than before, hungrier than before, fewer of them and less ammunition—and again the Chinese charging upward and defeat for General Sung.

There was a difference. The Chinese overran many positions. But Captain Barber, wounded again and still at his post, sent out the word: "Nobody above ground." The Marines stayed below. They had scooped recesses in the sides of their holes. They hid there while Chinese roved their "captured" battlefield and they shot upward or at an angle at anything that moved.

So they hung on, by half an eyelash now, for there were hardly ninety of them left to fight.

General Sung fared no better at Hagaru. Three attacks planned for that night failed to develop in anything like force.

Lieutenant Colonel Ridge's Korean line-crossers had come back with the straight dope again. It was to be more of the same: massed assaults on Item and How Companies, the knockout blow for East Hill.

But they were broken up before they got started. Marine artillery and mortars made an uninhabitable hell of the Chinese assembly areas. And Marine air got in its first good licks at night. Night hecklers on station in the darkness were guided to their targets by a fiery X of crisscrossing machine-gun tracers.

Scorched and scattered, unable to assemble, the Chinese crept back to their huts and hideouts.

Beside The Road in Hell-Fire Valley, the Chinese were creeping downhill for the kill. Success had at last crowned their tactics of isolation and piecemeal destruction. Though Drysdale and Sitter had been able to get about

300 men into Hagaru, the living and able survivors of the 900 men who had left Koto that morning—about 450 troops—had been fragmented into quarters.

These four fragments were strung out in Hell-Fire Valley along a 1,600-yard line running south from a point halfway between Hagaru and Koto-ri. First Fragment, the closest to Hagaru, was composed of about 130 Marine headquarters and service troops and soldiers from Baker Company. Second Fragment was composed of about 140 men of Baker Company, the 41st Commando, and Marine headquarters. Third Fragment was Major Seeley's 30 or 40 motor-men, mail clerks, and oddments from division headquarters. Fourth Fragment was the tank rear guard and tank reinforcements, about 100 men and more than a dozen tanks.

To the front of all four fragments, that burning British ammunition truck and other wrecked vehicles formed an impassable barrier above which lay the defile held by the Chinese. And all four fragments were separated by gaps of from 200 to 400 yards into which groups of Chinese had infiltrated. Thus the enemy had sealed Hell-Fire Valley front and rear and had chopped 450 men and about 100 vehicles into four pieces.

Major John McLaughlin had taken charge of First Fragment, for Lieutenant Colonel Arthur Chidester and other officers senior to him had been wounded in the early enemy onslaught. McLaughlin rallied his men and deployed them in covered-wagon fashion behind the stalled vehicles.

Second Fragment did the same, as did Major Seeley with Third Fragment. Farthest south, Fourth Fragment's tanks swung around to blast their way out of the trap and return to Koto-ri.

But the other Fragments continued to battle from road-side ditches and from behind their truck barricades. They fired into the Chinese moving cautiously over the low ground to either side of them. Casualties mounted steadily. Ammunition dwindled. Small parties were cut off and destroyed or captured by groups of Chinese infiltrators. Some of the Second Fragment's men slipped off into the darkness to line up with Major Seeley's Third Fragment. Others joined McLaughlin. Many more were killed or captured, or escaped into the hills to seek refuge and the hope of rescue in mountain caves or to perish in the snow. Second Fragment disappeared.

Now there were just First and Third Fragments. Each was girded in a ring of fire, two blazing circles steadily shrinking as the Chinese drew closer. Well past midnight of November 29, the Chinese brought up machine guns and began firing down the ditches where most of the wounded lay. Wounds were added to wounds. Warrant Officer Lloyd Dirst, who had been roaming the lines of the First Fragment, passing out ammunition and directing fire, fell with a severe head wound. Sergeant James Nash, hit himself, having already rescued two wounded buddies under fire, slipped out into the flashing night to drag him back. Heroism had become the common denominator, and now there was another one—shortage of ammunition.

McLaughlin's men had beaten back two Chinese charges, but they were down to a clip of ammunition per man—eight bullets apiece. They were firing carefully, listening for movement, searching for shadows. The Chinese mortar fire slackened, grew silent. Only desultory shots could be heard.

Out of the blackness came an American voice, shouting: "Major McLaughlin! Major McLaughlin!"

All the firing seemed to fall off at once, and a hush fell on the valley.

"Who's there?" McLaughlin called out.

"Sergeant Tovar. I'm a prisoner. They want to talk to you."

McLaughlin considered. He could hear the moaning of his wounded and could finger the last clip of bullets for his carbine.

"Come in and be identified," he shouted.

Sergeant Guillermo Tovar passed through the Marine lines and made his way to McLaughlin. The Marine commander talked to him and instructed him to bring the Chinese negotiators to the roadside. He met them there— three men, among them an English-speaking Chinese officer—and he could not resist a certain temptation.

"Have you come to surrender?" he asked.

The spokesman was not impressed.

"You surrender," he replied evenly. "We have many men and we have you surrounded. You lay down your arms and your wounded can go back to Koto-ri."

McLaughlin replied that he would have to confer with Chidester. He returned to him. With so little ammunition, they could not hope to fight much longer. They couldn't attempt a breakout and leave their wounded.

"Can we trust them with the wounded?" Chidester asked.

McLaughlin shrugged. "That's the chance we'd have to take."

Chidester gave his consent, and McLaughlin returned, hoping to stall the Chinese for as long as possible on the slim chance that air support might appear. He came up to the spokesman and pointed down The Road.

"I'll have to talk to the commander of the other unit," he said.

The spokesman shook his head. "No. You stay here." He pointed at Sergeant Tovar. "He can go." McLaughlin concealed his disappointment, drew Tovar aside and said: "Stall. Take your time." Tovar nodded. Accompanied by the other Chinese, he made his way down to Major Seeley.

And Seeley, too, was clinging to the hope of salvation from the skies. Meeting Tovar, he told him: "I'm going to stall. I've got more ammo than McLaughlin. If we can hold out until daylight, we can chase these bastards out of here with Marine air. I'm not going to surrender."

Led by Tovar, he approached the two Chinese. One of them began to gesticulate in sign language, for the English-speaking spokesman had stayed with McLaughlin. He pointed at Seeley. He threw his weapon to the ground. He raised his hands above his head. Then, jabbing an impatient thumb at Seeley, he held up three fingers.

Seeley pretended not to understand.

Exasperated, the Chinese repeated his dumb show. When he had concluded, he held up a warning hand. Two fingers.

Seeley got the message. But though he could stall no longer, he could still refuse to surrender. He made his decision plain, turned, and strode back into the darkness.

The Chinese shrugged stoically and returned with Tovar to their English-speaking comrade and McLaughlin. The major was stalling, too, but the spokesman's patience was also wearing thin.

"You must surrender," he repeated irritably. "We have you surrounded and we have killed and wounded many of you. If you don't surrender, we will kill you all."

"What about our wounded?" McLaughlin countered. "If they're left out in the cold they'll die. They have to go back to Koto."

The Chinese put their heads together before the spokes-man said: "We will take care of them."

"You must promise," McLaughlin insisted. "We are not going to surrender because you've beaten us. We're surrendering to get help for our wounded."

"We promise," the spokesman replied, and McLaughlin agreed to surrender.

Sadly, some of them weeping openly, the Marines laid down their arms. And then there was a wild scuffling of feet in the darkness, a jabbering of voices, and scores of white-coated figures swarmed onto the road—not to fall upon the defenseless Americans, but to pounce upon the trucks. They tore through the supplies in a frenzy, laugh-ing with delight or chattering with excitement whenever they came upon anything to eat or wear. Only after they had sated themselves did they turn to their prisoners with anything like interest. One of them ran toward Sergeant Nash, his arm uplifted.

"Here it is," the sergeant thought bitterly, bracing himself for the blow. "Now it starts."

But the Chinese hand descended on Nash's shoulder in a friendly pat. The soldier was speaking warmly, trying to make English words. Nash could make out, "Friend . . . comrade . . . Communist comrade. . . ." As he and the other prisoners would learn, their captors confidently ex-pected to convert them. But the smiles and soft words would shortly disappear along the long road back to the Yalu, once the Communists found that the Marines were not anxious to repent of wrongs committed in the name of Capitalism. Those hands smoothed to stroke would soon be clenched to strike. And Nash and dozens like him would be planning their escape.

Among them would be Pfc. Charles Kaylor. So far

from being home for Christmas 1950, he would not make Minneapolis until June of 1951.

Nor would the Chinese keep their promise to care for the wounded. Most of them were taken north, many of whom, such as Lieutenant Colonel Chidester, died of wounds en route or in prison camp. A handful of the most seriously wounded were left in roadside huts, there to face the cruel Korean winter on canteens of water and a few cups of food.

And down at the tail Major Seeley was slipping out of the trap. In the lull which had fallen on Hell-Fire Valley, he had rounded up his men, collected his wounded, and struck off over the mountains on an exhausting five-hour march to Koto. Throughout the day of November 30, stragglers stumbled into the friendly lines in both directions.

So ended the ordeal of Task Force Drysdale.

It had lost 162 men killed or missing in action, 159 wounded, and 321 captured or otherwise put out of action. Of its 150 vehicles, 75 were lost. But the point had made Hagaru, bringing a dozen tanks and 300 battle-seasoned troops to that beleaguered bastion.

The fight at Hell-Fire Valley had gone to General Sung. But it would cost him Hagaru.

CHAPTER TWELVE

IT WAS November 30. The turning point was approaching. At Yudam-ni, the turning movement was beginning.

Litzenberg and Murray had met in their council of war. They had made plans to execute General Smith's order to shift from a left-to-right position to a fore-and-aft line. That wall of men and arms would swing round into a battering-ram that would punch southward down The Road when the breakout began next day. Litzenberg's Seventh would be its head, Murray's Fifth its tail. Neither position would be more or less honorable, more or less hot, than the other, for this was going to be nothing less than a fighting perimeter on the march, and there would be fighting on every side.

Before the turn began, the two regimental commanders threw together another of those composite battalions, another patchwork made of a remnant of this company, a rag of that. It would hold high ground while the Seventh drove south.

Major Maurice Roach took command of it. Being possessed of a sardonic sense of humor, he named his hodge-

podge the "Damnation Battalion." Being a believer in
esprit, he searched for a distinguishing badge that would
bind the Damnation boys together, make them proud of
their new outfit. He found a man wearing a hank of green
parachute silk around his neck. Finding more green silk,
he ordered it cut up and issued as scarves.

Sporting their green neckerchiefs, the men of the Damnation Battalion climbed and held their hill while the
Seventh slugged to the south and the Fifth swung into line.

It was an amazingly orderly movement. It almost went
unchallenged. Litzenberg and Murray had decided to
make it in broad daylight, with the help of artillery and
air support. This was augmented at the only critical
moment by the Chinese passion for looting.

As one of the Fifth's units disengaged and pulled down
the reverse side of a hill, the Chinese came swarming up
the forward slope.

Had the Chinese pursued, had they fallen upon the
Marines' rear, they might have gotten down into the valley
with serious consequences. But they stopped to root among
piles of burning supplies the Marines had left behind.

So the turn was made. Ammunition and rations were
issued for the following day's action. Fresh supplies were
air-dropped. All superfluous equipment was carefully
destroyed. The dead were buried. A few more wounded
were evacuated, and all was made ready for the breakout.

One more day . . .

At Fox Hill Hector Cafferata gazed at his big toes
sticking out the ends of Iverson's cut-out boots, and wept.

Iverson had died. With plasma frozen and useless, the
corpsman had been helpless. Iverson had lost too much
blood from a hole a grenade had torn in his ribs. He had

known he was going, too. Only that morning he had said:
"Hey, Moose, when I die I want you to take my boots to
keep those canalboats of yours warm."

So he had died, and Cafferata had taken the boots, cut
holes in the ends and put them on. Now, looking at his
toes sticking out, thinking of Iverson, Cafferata was
crying.

It was quiet outside Item Company's lines at Hagaru,
although occasionally snipers would shoot from the far-
off slopes. Suddenly a Marine machine gunner leaped to
his feet, tugged his pistol from its holster, and emptied
it at the hillside. His buddies crowded around him, concerned, thinking him "shook." The Marine grinned.

"Aw, shit," he said. "I missed!"

Koto-ri had had its worst night of fire the night before.
The Chinese had come against the Second Battalion, First,
commanded by Lieutenant Colonel Allan Sutter, and they
had left 175 dead in the snow, pulling back with an estimated 200 wounded. Marine losses had been six killed,
eighteen wounded.

For some mysterious reason the Chinese were not hitting
hard at Koto. They seemed content to isolate it, to fortify
the hills above and below it. But Koto was becoming a
bastion, nevertheless, the most important point along The
Road, after Hagaru. A small airstrip had already been
built for the observation planes that were the eyes of the
division's artillery. A vital communications link was main-
tained with the forces at Hamhung and below, and Koto
continued to receive supplies against the day when the
division would break out of Hagaru and regroup for the
final thrust to the sea.

Even now, on this afternoon of November 30, parachutes were floating in the skies above the town, swaying
in the wind, falling with the weight of the supply cases
attached to them. Once a case of bullets fell free of its
parachute. It plunged through the roof of Sutter's headquarters tent. It dropped harmlessly among a group of
staff officers, striking the hard earth to bounce up on a
crate used for a table.

"Too bad it wasn't beans instead of bullets," one of
them said.

But there were other cases which *did* contain unwarlike
supplies. There were others that contained contraceptives.
The supply officer in Japan, perhaps not too clear about
the nature of warfare, as supply officers often are not,
had sent the boys a recreation package or two. They were
greeted with splendid hoots of derision. A few of them
were brought to Colonel Puller, and Chesty, chafing because most of the glory was to be found north of him,
eagerly seized this chance to add another Pullerism to the
other side of the legend. He pulled his pipe from his mouth
and growled:

"What the hell do they think we're doing to these
Chinese?"

Down at Chinhung-ni, the Communists were using cav-
alry. Horsemen had taken possession of a valley to the
left, or west, of the town's perimeter, and were fortifying
a village there. The Marines went out after them.

Two companies of Lieutenant Colonel Donald
Schmuck's First Battalion, First, attacked astride the
high ground. They were supported by mortars, artillery,
and a quartet of daring Marine pilots who swooped low

in the narrow valley to hammer at the Chinese. Once the supporting arms had punished the lowland fortifications, the Marines closed in from the high flanks to clean them out. Point after point was reduced in this way, and the battle ended with a group of mounted Chinese fleeing still farther westward, urging their shaggy Mongolian ponies on with sharp cries, and pursued by the delighted "Yip, yip—yippeees!" of their tormentors.

The Marines were counterattacking East Hill at Hagaru. The men of George Company, First, who had fought their way up from Hell-Fire Valley were now passing through the thin line held by Major Myers's force. They went upward at nine o'clock on the morning of November 30. Before dark they had thrown the Chinese out, regrouped, and dug in.

But the enemy could be expected back.

Hagaru's commander, Lieutenant Colonel Ridge, was certain of it. So was General Smith, sitting in his headquarters where he had passed the day in conferences with the commanders of Tenth Corps. But he was optimistic about the result, for now they had the tanks, Captain Sitter's men atop the hill, and Drysdale's Royal Marines in reserve.

Both his expectations and confidence were justified. The enemy did hit hard at East Hill that night. But they were contained in a wild fight. Sitter himself was wounded by a grenade. He rejected evacuation and held the line. At one point Chinese shells struck a dump of gasoline drums, setting them afire. In the light of the flames, General Smith stood in his doorway, watching the battle less than a mile away. And above the clamor he could hear the motors of the engineers, still working through the night to complete the airfield. It should be serviceable tomorrow, Partridge had said.

One more day, General Smith thought, one more day . . .

It had grown dark atop Fox Hill. It was quiet. The American warbirds had flown home to roost, and one of the last sights of the dying day had been the spectacle of that gallant little observation plane, buzzing boldly above the enemy while its pilot dropped hand grenades on them.

Now, it was black—and the night of November 30 wore on.

Suddenly four Chinese machine guns opened up from the rocky ridge above Fox Hill. They poured a harassing fire into the Marines. Though they killed or wounded no one, they murdered everyone's sleep.

Captain Barber decided to put an end to the nuisance of the ridge. He asked his artillery observer, Lieutenant Don Campbell, to contact How Battery in Hagaru. He ordered O'Leary to co-ordinate mortar illumination shells with How's 105 howitzer fire, so that Sergeant Clyde Pitts could observe the result with field glasses. Quickly Campbell radioed the enemy's position. How Battery replied:

"Four guns on your command."

O'Leary laid his mortars on. Sergeant Pitts lay in his hole and peered through his glasses. Campbell gave the order to How Battery:

"Fire!"

In an instant, How Battery reported: "Four rounds on the way."

O'Leary's mortars plopped from their tubes. Two shells burst with the arrival of the howitzer shells. Four more exploded. The rocky ridge was brilliantly outlined. Cap-

tain Barber began calling into his telephone to Sergeant
Pitts, asking for adjustments. His reply was an ecstatic
babble.

"Beautiful . . . beautiful . . . beeee—*yoo*—ti—full . . ."

"Goddamit, Pitts," Captain Barber yelled, "what about
those machine guns?"

" 'At's what I was sayin', sir. They're gone. Damned if
they didn't knock all four of 'em to hell an' gone with
the first salvo!"

Campbell jubilantly messaged Hagaru:

"Cease fire, target destroyed, mission accomplished."

There was an interval of stunned silence at the other
end. Then, tentatively, timidly, How Battery made its
request:

"Would you say again all after 'cease fire'?"

Grinning, Campbell obliged: "Target destroyed, mission accomplished."

There was another silence, and then a sharp, terminat-
ing click on the radio. How battery said nothing more.
Having said the impossible with a single salvo fired at
night from seven miles off, anything further would be
anticlimactic.

So Fox Hill passed the remainder of the night unmolested, its defenders praying for the strength to hold
out one more day.

One more day . . .

On the night of November 30, they all yearned for it,
prayed for it, from Chinhung-ni to Chosin Reservoir—
on the weather side of the ridges where the wind wailed
and cut like a ragged-edged knife and the men drew parachute silk around them for warmth . . . on the warmer
leeward slopes, in the valleys, the warming tents . . . in

the hospital tents where doctors worked with weary brains and fingers that were no longer nimble, where suffering men stirred and groaned softly and corpsmen brought coffee or morphine, where chaplains in helmets and parkas knelt beside the cots, only their moving lips and black books marking their calling . . . in the huts of Hell-Fire Valley where a handful of men lay in the bitter blackness, wondering what had happened, and where death had already laid an icy finger on blackening lips . . . along the frozen rim of Chosin Reservoir where the soldiers and South Koreans of Task Force Faith were huddled, clinging to the last hope of the one more day that would get them to Hagaru . . . "Give us this day," they prayed, "and also tomorrow . . ."

For Task Force Faith, there would be only tomorrow.

Dawn would come on December 1, and with it the beginning of the breakout at Yudam-ni, the formation of the relief column for Fox Hill, the arrival of air transports at Hagaru, the unleashing of full-scale Marine aerial assault. And this dawn would also signal the dissolution of Task Force Faith.

Like the men of Fox Hill, these three mixed battalions of the Army's Seventh Division had been hammered and hit since the first Chinese onslaught of November 27–28. Like the men of Task Force Drysdale, they had been cut in two. They had fought back together, supported by Far East Air Force and Marine planes. With the death of Colonel Allen MacLean, C.O. of the 31st Regiment, Lieutenant Colonel Faith had taken command and set up a defensive perimeter. This, too, had been battered, but there had been air drops of supplies and constant help from the skies. There had been hope, too, when an Army relieving force had been dispatched from Hagaru. But the Communists had hurled it back with heavy casualties and the loss of two tanks. On the night of November 30, Task Force Faith had girded for a breakout to Hagaru, hardly a half-dozen miles below.

With the dawn of December 1, Lieutenant Colonel Faith destroyed equipment, placed his numerous wounded aboard a convoy of trucks, and struck out.

Aerial support was magnificent. All morning long and throughout most of the afternoon, the planes screamed down from the skies, rocketing and blasting ridges packed with Chinese. Task Force Faith was getting closer to Hagaru.

Four and a half miles above it, the column was halted at a blown bridge. An attempt to cross on the ice was begun. The Chinese struck, attacking with infantry preceded by self-propelled guns. Faith rallied his men. But he fell at dusk, mortally wounded.

And there Task Force Faith fell apart.

There was no one to take command, there was the futility of command among so many men who spoke no English and who had no experience of discipline under fire. The unit's N.C.O.'s fought valiantly, struggling to ward off utter destruction. But with darkness Task Force Faith had ceased to exist. It was in fragments. Its survivors were in the hills, leaderless, demoralized, groups of stragglers drawn together by the misery of a common catastrophe, all dragging themselves over ice and snow and bound for the sanctuary of Hagaru.

Behind them, beside the ice, silent and immobile, lay the trucks filled with wounded.

CHAPTER THIRTEEN

AT DAWN on December 1—that same dawn which had lighted Task Force Faith to its disastrous dusk— the Marines of Yudam-ni were preparing for the breakout that was supposed to be impossible.

For no one in the world, except those Marines and their commanders, seemed to think it possible. Least of all did General Sung Shin-lun. Battered though he might be, General Sung still had plenty left, more fresh divisions with which to replace the exhausted ones—and he still held the high ground along The Road.

In Washington the Joint Chiefs of Staff considered the breakout impossible. They were writing off the First Marine Division, just as that division had been written off eight years before, during the dark days of Guadalcanal.

In the States newspapers were chanting a gaudy requiem and editorial writers were angrily flaying everyone but the Communist Chinese for the disaster then impending.

In MacArthur's headquarters they were sad and grieving, sad because things did look very black, grieving because the blame for having sacrificed a famous Marine division would certainly fall on them.

In Hungnam the Americans were burning supplies. The Navy was preparing for the fighting evacuation of Tenth Corps.

So it was impossible. It had to be so, by every logic of numbers, terrain, and weather. But such a logic merely menaces the head. It lets the heart beat free. Such a logic persuades the timorous, convinces the rational, but cannot bind the bold.

And this was a bold division, born in defeat, bred to adversity, led by an optimist, and even more emboldened by the knowledge that Chosin's skies would belong to men of their own breed, riding the cockpits of Marine fighters.

Marine air would break them out, break every one of General Sung's clutching fingers until he at last let go.

Rarely, if ever before, had military success depended so much on a supporting arm. But never before during a time of total air superiority had weather and terrain done so much to balk that support.

There was intermittent snow, flurrying or whirling in blizzards. There was a sullen low overcast, enshrouding the jagged mountain peaks in swirling mists. Altimeters gave no warning of these. Yet this was close aerial support. The fighters had to come in low, rocketing, bombing, and strafing within as few as twenty-five yards of their own men. They had to fly beneath the overcast or strike down through it, wisps of cloud curling alongside, and then, suddenly, abruptly, the earth, the target, the looming mountain mass. They had to fly down valleys and ravines. Coming in low, they lost speed, were vulnerable to enemy ground fire.

All the while they had to look for those colored panels

that marked the Marine line to avoid killing their own
men. Frequently they attacked in a compass circle. Four
planes dived on a target from the four points of the
compass, one after the other, often interspersing their
assaults with dummy runs that would keep the enemy
down as well as conserve ammunition. A dummy run
might also set up the Chinese for the following assault,
which, with flaming guns and swishing rockets, would be
terribly real. On station during the day, they were directed to their targets by the Forward Air Controllers,
those aviators who were assigned to the infantry units and
were linked to them by radio. Sometimes they were guided
by an aerial control point established in a transport. At
night they dived at positions marked out for them by the
X of crossing tracers or the white puff of phosphorous
shells or were talked on target by the FAC's.

*"Hello, Firefly Six, this is Arson One Four. We're
getting mortar fire. Position southeast Yudam-ni, repeat
—southeast."*

*"Wilco Arson One Four. Firefly Six is on the way.
Out."*

*Below, standing in a jeep, probably exposed to enemy
fire, the FAC keeps talking him in.*

*"I hear your motors, Firefly Six. Blink your lights.
Okay, you're coming right over us. You're on course. We'll
give you some white phosphorous."*

"Wilco. I will orbit."

*The pilot turns his craft, coming in again, peering
through the dark for the little puff of white that will mark
his target. There it is! He flips his arming switches, starts
down. But there's another! Another. The Chinese are
canny. They're exploding their own white phosphorous
shells.*

"Hello, Arson One Four. The Goo-Goos are fouling up the detail. They're unloading their own WP. Get me some tracers while I orbit again."

"Roger. Wilco."

Again the plane turns, again the arming switches are flipped. Now the pinpricks of light, like lines of tiny red hyphens, go flashing out to mark their X. The flier swoops down with flaming rockets and stuttering 20mm guns.

"That did it, Firefly Six. Nice goin'—and come back any time."

Thus the night. Back at Yonpo Airfield or aboard the carrier Baedong Strait, mechanics worked on engines with bared and frozen fingers. If the weather was bad for flying, it was worse for maintenance. The terrible cold of this bleak and blasted land mocked at Western man while laying a cold, immobilizing hand on his chief advantage, his machinery.

At Yonpo, without heated hangar space, engines were freezing. Even diluted oil would not stay fluid. Like the tankers and truckers on The Road, air crewmen had to run the engines every two hours to prevent their freezing. Bomb handling equipment also froze. Bomb trucks running around the clock between Yonpo and the supply depots to the north at Hungnam dumped their loads merely by driving out from under them. The bombs tumbled in clattering heaps, into jumbles of enormous, drab-hued jellybeans. They were rolled to the bomb trailers, tugged and pushed aboard, and then the trailers were dragged by hand beneath the yawning bellies of the waiting planes. There the bombs were lifted up to the racks with straining stomach muscles and legs and shoulders that were aching and shrieking in an agony of protest. It was labor at its most menial level, and it made these trained technicians aware of the harsh irony that had cracked and split the veneer of their skills, reducing them to the level of the "backward" enemy.

"Where are the push buttons?" the ground crews sneered, seizing shovels or contriving rude plows to clear the airfield of snow that had packed its surface and made it beautifully white and perilously smooth.

And there was always a shortage of spare parts. Stocks were mainly replenished by cannibalizing planes which had crashed near the airfield or by mounting armed excursions to scavenge those shot down in no man's land.

But these toiling ground crews would keep their squadrons airborne, keep them flying north to strike at the flanks, rear and front of the fighting perimeter that would be on the march from Yudam-ni.

Breakout began at eight o'clock on the morning of December 1. At that moment all initiative in the Chosin Reservoir campaign had passed to the First Marine Division. But first the Marines buried the last of their dead.

Fourscore bodies in sleeping bags or swathed in blankets were placed in a shallow excavation, each spaced a few paces from the next. Men who had often risked their lives to retrieve those frozen corpses had stood silently on the hilltops to watch or had gathered in the valley, gazing at chaplains of all faiths moving between the rows, listening to the low hurried murmur of their prayers, feeling the tears freeze on their cheeks. Each time the prayer was ended, the chaplain nodded and the dirt was shoved back into place. At last there were no more bodies visible. There was only the dark earth, and soon this too would be white with snow. The valley mourners returned to their lines and a map was made of the grave's location.

Meanwhile Colonel Litzenberg and Lieutenant Colonel Murray conferred in the last council of war at Yudam-ni. They had already formulated a threefold plan.

First, they would disengage—let loose of the tiger's tail.

Second, they would throw the Chinese off two high mountain peaks sitting at either side of The Road three miles below the town.

Third, they would reinforce Fox Hill by a dramatic overland march.

Of this last Litzenberg had said: "They think we're roadbound. They think we'll stick with our vehicles. And they won't except us to attack at night."

Murray had agreed, and Lieutenant Colonel Raymond Davis's First Battalion, Seventh, had been chosen to relieve Fox Hill. With dusk, after the capture of the twin peaks, Davis's men would ascend the eastern one and strike off over trackless snows to join the beleaguered force still clinging to the hill commanding Toktong Pass.

Since dawn the artillerymen had been "destroying" their excess ammunition. They rid themselves of it by firing at the enemy. They plastered the ridges with a fearful barrage. Then, with skeleton crews manning the guns, the rest of them formed into infantry platoons.

It was eight o'clock, the breakout was beginning.

In the hills to the north two battalions of Marines prepared to let loose of the tiger's tail.

South, one battalion of Marines made the approach march to the twin peaks.

At the bridge below the town a party of engineers fixed their charges of explosive.

In the valley of Yudam-ni a lone tank clanked to the head of a long column of men and vehicles—a column which would stretch and coil for miles along that mountain road. Its warhead was the tank and supporting arms and troops. Its highland flanks were the battalions which would take to the hills and seize high point after high point. Its lowland flanks were the riflemen marching to either side, clearing the brush of enemy. Its vertical flank —the skies—were those swooping and growling Marine Corsairs. Its rear was the heavier howitzers, which, if halted, would not block the line of march. Its center was the trucks loaded with supplies, loaded with wounded, and those "cracker-box" ambulances also clogged with wounded. For no one but the wounded or the frostbitten rode in this column. Tarpaulins had been placed over the supplies, and atop these the casualties had been placed. Even the men who "rode shotgun" in the cabins or on the tailgates were men who could not walk but could still fight. And the walking wounded marched beside the vehicles, rifles at the ready. Not even the commanders rode, for their jeeps were stuffed with wounded. Litzenberg walked. Murray walked. And so the column formed, and came out fighting.

In the hills to the north the tail was coming down—by trickery and stealth.

Trickery worked for George Company, Fifth. Close to the enemy, within grenade range, they called for a dummy run of Corsairs while they began pulling back. The planes came roaring down. The Chinese took cover. George Company's men began leaving their holes. They started downhill. The Chinese scrambled to their feet and came swarming in. The Corsairs returned. But the Chinese were not to be fooled twice. They rushed on. The Corsairs let go. As the Marines gained the valley, the hill they had abandoned seemed to erupt. It was not only the Corsairs'

Napalm and rockets, or even the mortars and artillery which had also ranged in; it was also the stores of ammunition to which George Company's men had thoughtfully fixed timed charges before pulling out.

Stealth came to the assistance of Baker Company, Fifth, the last rear guard. Though its commander bore the name of John Hancock, he forsook flamboyance for subtlety. He requested that his outfit receive no supporting fire. They sneaked off the hill, using only light machine-gun fire to rake those Chinese who were drawn up to it by that curious silence.

So the tail was pulled out of town, while Marine engineers gleefully blew the bridge out of sight. It was three o'clock in the afternoon.

By three o'clock in the afternoon, the airfield at Hagaru was ready.

It was by no means completed. It was far less than the manuals required. It had only 2,900 feet of prepared surface and 4,000 feet of cleared surface, but Lieutenant Colonel Partridge had pronounced it ready, and now a two-motored C-47 transport was carefully letting down for a landing.

It came in safely. It came in to the wild cheering of those engineers who had built the field in less than two weeks, to the satisfaction of the commanding general who had envisioned it, and to the relief of the officer who had directed its construction.

"Sir," Lieutenant Colonel Partridge reported to Major General Smith, "I have a deep sense of well-being."

Immediately the evacuation of the wounded commenced. Some one hundred of them were taken out; then, just

before dark, the fourth plane to arrive cracked up at the
end of the strip. It was a Marine transport loaded with
ammunition. But the wreckage was cleared, and the engineers again set to work under floodlights, improving the
landing field for the next day's traffic.

Hagaru was no longer cut off.

Fox Hill still was. On this December 1, the fifth day of
encirclement, the men spoke confidently to each other of
relief, swearing that they'd soon get off that miserable
mountain. To themselves they were not so sure. There were
only about eighty of them now. There was less ammunition. Food stocks were way down, and it was getting to be
an ordeal to gather all that snow for so little water. Sometimes men would take a five-gallon can down to The Road,
where a tiny spring still defied the cold and bubbled with
fresh water. They did it under sniper fire from the rocky
ridge above, but they got the water.

Pfc. Benson went down, sliding and bumping half the
way. He filled the can. He placed it on his shoulder and
started up, stooping to clutch at bushes for handholds.

There was a shot. There was a loud clanging beside
Benson's ear, and then water spouted from holes in either
side of the can. It drenched him. The can clattered back
down the hill.

Infuriated, his parka already stiffening with ice, Benson scrambled up the hill, seized another can, and started
down again. He filled it, clasped it to his chest, and
screamed: "Shoot, you slant-eyed son of a bitch! Only
you're gonna have to get both of us this time!"

He got back up with the water, and until darkness fell,
the men of Fox Hill would have another piece of grim
comedy to sustain them.

The twin peaks below Yudam-ni were very tough. The Chinese were there in strength. They were dug in. Aerial support was not enough to flush them out. Nor could mortar and artillery fire shake them loose. Foot-sloggers had to go in with rifles and grenades. They attacked, drenched in the sweat of their climb up the mountainside. By the late afternoon of December 1, one company had gained the crest of Hill 1542, the westward peak and the highest. But the Chinese hurled them off again. By dark the Marines held only the roadside slope of Hill 1542.

On the other side of The Road, the peak known as Hill 1419 was taken, but only after Davis's battalion had been committed to the assault. Now these men and the How Company, Seventh, which had hit the hill before them, having marched and fought since dawn, turned their faces toward Fox Hill.

It lay about three miles straight to the southeast of them. But Lieutenant Colonel Davis was not moving toward Fox Hill as the crow flies. His first objective was Hill 1520, a Chinese-held peak about 2,500 yards directly south of him. From Hill 1520, he would wheel directly east to assault another Chinese mountaintop the same distance away. This was Hill 1653. From Hill 1653 directly south to Fox Hill was a distance of about 3,000 yards. Thus something closer to five miles of unknown mountain country lay between Davis's men and their final objective.

Davis began to move swiftly. He knew that his men had been fighting almost constantly since November 10. They were approaching the limit of their endurance. Worse, it was getting fearfully cold. By nightfall, it was already 16 degrees below zero, and would fall to 24 below before morning. Davis could not risk having his men freeze in their own sweat. He set them to work forming a temporary perimeter, evacuating the dead and wounded to The Road below. It would take hours. He could not wait for the litter-bearers to return. He sent only those least able to continue, the most exhausted and the walking wounded. These men would care for the battalion's heavy gear, drive the trucks when the regimental train moved out.

Nor could Davis take many supporting arms, for he had already abandoned his plan of probing with patrols before swinging the main body around the enemy's flanks. This, too, would take too long, already some of the men squatted in eight inches of snow, half stupefied. No, they would advance in single file, with flankers twenty yards to either side. So he took only two heavy mortars and six machine guns, manning them with double crews. Litters were used to carry ammunition. Each man carried an extra mortar shell and an extra bandoleer of ammunition. For food there was four days' rations, chiefly cans of fruit, for they would not freeze and the sugar gave quick energy. They also carried sleeping bags, either to protect the wounded or to guard against exposure should they be cut off in the hills. Thus encumbered, each man was bent beneath a load of over a hundred pounds, when at 9 o'clock on the night of December 1, Davis gave the word to move out.

It was dark, but a few stars winked coldly over the horizon. Davis would guide on these, as well as the larger rock masses. And artillery had been instructed to drop white phosphorous shells on the peaks.

But in the valleys the stars could not be seen. Peaks viewed from on high displayed changed profiles when seen below. Or else they all looked alike. The tiny puffs of the

phosphorous shells were almost impossible to detect. Time
after time Davis got down into a hole to consult his compass. He pulled a poncho over his head and switched on
his flashlight. Somehow, the column always seemed off
course. That maddening tendency to veer to the right had
taken hold of his point.

The relief column moved with agonizing slowness. Men
in the point were breaking trail through snow up to their
knees. They floundered in drifts. Men following them
trampled the snow, packing it smooth and slippery for
those in the rear. They slipped and fell, raising a chilling
clatter in the darkness with helmets clanging against rifle
muzzles. So jolted, frozen joints ached and groaned as
though stretched on a rack. Each time a man fell, he was
slower regaining his feet. Litter-bearers lost their balance,
spilling the shells. They had to be retrieved from the snow.

They pressed on, a long wavering line of dark lumps
creeping up this ridge, down into the next valley, up the
next knob, and down again—sliding, staggering, digging
their heels into the snow to break their momentum.

They were ascending a ridge about halfway to Hill
1520 when long-range fire raked them from the right
flank. Davis paused. He forced his numbed brain to think.
The Road was off to the right. Perhaps the fire was from
forces engaged there. But could he be that close? The
half mile or so between his line of march and The Road
had been interdicted for Marine artillery fire. Davis attempted to contact his leading unit, his point, about a
quarter mile ahead of him. He wanted to tell the men to
halt at the next ridge lying beneath the crest of Hill 1520.
They were too far to the right.

But Davis's radio had gone dead. He tried passing the
word by voice. The men couldn't hear. Ears muffled in ice-

encrusted parkas were powerless to hear. They plodded
ahead, unheeding.

Davis was alarmed. More and more fire came from the
right. He could see tracers. He could see his guiding star
again, and the gap widening between this and the dark
finger of the point ahead, veering right, ever right.

They were heading straight for that no man's land
covered by Marine artillery. If they reached it, friendly
fire might fall on them.

Davis stumbled ahead. He outdistanced his runner and
his radioman. That single dreadful consideration took
possession of his brain, driving him on past staggering
men who cursed him softly as he brushed by them, knock-
ing them off balance or upsetting their loads. They
couldn't recognize him. If they had, it could not have
altered that dull resentment. Now Davis had ceased to
think. What drove him on had been lost in the frozen
wastes of his mind. He wanted only to reach the point.
Once there, he would force that block of ice within his
head to surrender the reason. All of his being had been
sunk in moving muscle of thigh and leg, in brittle bone
and wavering ankle. He stumbled on until, an hour later,
he at last overhauled the point.

He overtook them just as they had reached a saddle in
the highest ground. In ten more minutes they might have
slogged on to disaster. It was midnight.

Again his will pointed a pistol at his brain and he
became conscious of thought. He halted his men to correct
the westward drift. The column moved out again. On the
east, or leftward slope of 1520, he halted his men to
reorganize. A following company swung around to the left
to build a perimeter. They blundered upon about two

dozen Chinese, asleep in foxholes. The enemy was motionless. Perhaps some of them were frozen dead. In their
quilted clothing they had wedged themselves in holes only
big enough to contain a single body.

The Marines saw them and did not kill them. They were
powerless to consider any enemy other than the cold. They
were mindless hulks of frozen flesh and bone, and here
were other hulks, reclining while they stood. The Marines
began to sink into the snow.

Somewhere someone could think. Word went back to
Lieutenant Colonel Davis that the enemy had been contacted. He gathered another force to come around the hill
in the opposite direction. He seized men bodily and hissed,
"What's your outfit?"

They gazed back at him blankly, stupidly. They didn't
know. If they did, they might not have been able to
answer.

He found an entire platoon sitting in the snow like
frozen Buddhas. They were in a state of coma. He shook
them, cuffed them, got them to their feet. He gave orders,
and then, because his own brain was sliding into that
seductive, mindless mist, he ordered them to repeat them.
He wanted to be sure they had heard, he wanted to be sure
he had spoken.

Firing broke out to the left. Grenades exploded. The
Marines had shaken out of their coma and were attacking
the high ground of Hill 1520. They weaved in like ghosts,
firing and hurling their charges. Now mortars were coming to their aid. It had taken the mortarmen ten minutes
to get into action—ten minutes to commence what normally required ten seconds. Bullets were striking in the
snow around Davis, around the comatose platoon. They

did not stir. They sat there, gazing vacantly at the snow spurting about them. The rest of the column was stumbling up the slopes behind.

The firing on the left died down. The Marines had routed the Chinese, taken the high ground—and now, an hour after Davis had reached the head of his column, the last of his men were climbing the crest of Hill 1520.

They came up, silently, mechanically, one after the other, and as soon as they reached the crest, they toppled. They fell into the snow with the horrible regularity of targets in a shooting gallery. And they lay there.

Again Davis and his officers and noncoms stumbled among the supine figures—slapping, pleading, cursing, cuffing—bringing them to their senses and their feet, for now the Chinese emplaced on lower ridges to their southern front were opening up again.

By three o'clock Davis's Marines had formed a perimeter atop Hill 1520. It was a tight circle with small company patrols to make the rounds. They sat down and waited for dawn while Davis made futile attempts to contact Fox Hill

It was a terrible night. Twice its blackness was pierced by the babbling screams of men who were losing their minds. Two Marines went insane that night. They were overpowered, subdued in strait jackets improvised from parkas, and placed on stretchers. With the dawn they would be carried forward—but they would not live.

At dawn Lieutenant Colonel Davis saw the rocky promontory above Fox Hill. Again he tried to make contact. Again he failed. And the air and artillery radios also were dead.

An hour after daylight, replenished by fruit or dry biscuits and two hours of fitful sleep, the column moved

east to Hill 1653. And the hills before them erupted with
enemy small-arms fire. The Chinese were firing from four
different knobs. Davis answered with long-range machine-
gun and mortar fire. One of the mortars quit. It was spiked
and buried. They would leave nothing to the Chinese.

Men were being hit. The opening bursts of enemy fire
killed three and wounded nine. The dead were buried. The
wounded were placed on stretchers. The Marines moved
against the enemy again. They leapfrogged to the attack,
taking knob after knob. They went up Hill 1653 and took
it.

The Chinese shifted their fire to the right flank and
rear. Still taking casualties, the column drove toward
Fox Hill 3,000 yards away.

Now it was 600 yards away. Davis could see it. He
could see the Marine defenders on its slopes. He drew his
rear in closer and marched on. Suddenly his radioman
was shouting: "Colonel! Colonel! Fox Hill on the radio!"
He was shaking with emotion. He was crying.

It was Captain Barber's voice on the radio.

"If you need help," he was saying, "we can send a patrol
out to you."

Lieutenant Colonel Davis smiled. It was not flamboyant,
this offer of help from the rescued to the rescuer. It was
the way they fought, the way Marines fight. Davis de-
clined, and Barber, with two fighters on station above him,
called them down in a fury upon Davis's exposed flank and
rear. In that interval, Davis ordered his B Company to
close on Fox Hill.

They ran.

They sprinted through the snow with a speed that
seemed to mock the awful night that had passed, and they
burst into Fox Company's lines with shouts and grins.

Two hours later, still bearing their wounded, all of the relief column would be within the defenses of Fox Hill. The saviors would gaze upon the saved, and both would conclude that the other was pretty beat.

One ordeal would have matched another, and thus would Fox Hill be relieved.

CHAPTER FOURTEEN

THEY had been drifting into Hagaru all night.

Since dusk on December 1, the stragglers from Task Force Faith had been streaming into the perimeter from the outlying hills.

The first arrivals had appeared just as day was dying. They had been stopped and questioned by Lieutenant Colonel Beall. He had made sure of their identity, then guided them through a mine field. Many more had followed, all through the night, stumbling into Hagaru with the dragging shuffle of the living dead. By twos, threes, dozens, they had come in, strangely bound by nation and rank—Americans with Americans, South Koreans with South Koreans, and after this, junior officer with junior officer, private with private, noncom joined to noncom. They had been directed to the rear, to warming tents hastily provided for them. Many of them were frostbitten. They had been ticketed for evacuation next day.

So they had come in, and now it was the morning of December 2. Lieutenant Colonel Beall had been told that there were many wounded in a truck convoy halted beside the frozen Reservoir. He drove north in a jeep to the edge of the ice two miles above the perimeter. With him were his driver, Pfc. Ralph Milton, Hospital Corpsman Oscar Biebinger, and Corporal Andrew Contreras of Motor Transport.

They stopped. Beall walked onto the ice. He tested it. It was solid. It had to be. With morning, the temperature had gone no higher than zero. He felt the cold seeping up through his boots and shivered. He was fifty-two years old and he had never been so cold in his life.

Beall and his Marines drove onto the ice. They had gone about a quarter mile toward the opposite shore, when they saw a half-dozen American soldiers on the ice. The Marines made for them. Communists on the opposite shore opened fire on their jeep. The Marines stopped. They crawled to the soldiers. They were all wounded, many of them with multiple wounds or broken bones. The Marines grasped two of them and stood erect to carry them back to the jeep. Again the Chinese fired. Beall and his men flopped onto the ice. They slid the wounded around, and then, rolling over on their backs, they got their hands under the helpless soldiers' armpits, drew them half onto their stomachs, and propelled themselves toward the jeep by pushing their heels against the ice. Once they had reached the jeep, the Communists ceased firing. The Marines stood up. They loaded their jeep with the wounded men and drove back to the friendly shore.

Now Beall organized a rescue. The wounded soldiers had told him they were from the truck convoy. There were many more stricken men out on the ice. They had wandered out there, or been driven there by the enemy, after the grenading of the casualty trucks. Some of the wounded had attempted to beat the Communists back, and the Chinese had responded by hurling grenades into their midst. They was why so many men had multiple wounds, why their hands were mangled. They had tried to throw the potato mashers out, and they had exploded in their hands. Sometimes the Chinese gave them cigarettes before shoving them toward the ice. Sometimes they fired at them as they staggered away. There were many more men out there, many—and there were parties of badly wounded holed up in Korean villages.

Beall called for trucks and jeep ambulances for another rescue trip. These were brought by Second Lieutenant Robert Hunt. Warming tents were erected back from the shore. Fires were started. Beall and his three men drove out on the ice again.

Again the Communists fired on them. They found that they could only advance at a crawl, that they had to leave their jeep at mid-ice. If they stood up to carry a wounded man to the jeep, bullets spattered around them chipping the ice. They crawled. They crawled during the morning, afternoon, and early night, bellies pressed against the snow-covered ice, leaving wriggling trails behind them like monster snow serpents. They made sleds of parkas. They rolled a wounded man on a parka and dragged him to the jeep. They found that they could crawl within 150 yards of the enemy, so long as they carried no weapons, did not come erect. Once Beall found a soldier with both legs badly broken. He had a serious shoulder wound. Beall took a sling from an abandoned rifle, looped it under the man's good shoulder and dragged him to safety. All the while Milton and Biebinger and Contreras worked with him. Now Hunt joined them. Once a stranger crawled onto the ice.

"Get back," Beall snapped. "Too many people out here
will draw their fire." He glared at the man. "What's your
outfit, anyway—what's your rank?"

"John Q. Civilian," the man replied. "My name's
LeFevre, and I'm the Red Cross field director in these
parts."

"What the hell're you doing here?"

The man shrugged. Beall shrugged.

"Okay. Stay."

LeFevre worked with the Marines until midafternoon,
when he collapsed and had to be dragged from the ice
himself.

Now there were bullock carts plodding down the ice
from the northern villages. They held nineteen wounded,
the men who had hidden in the huts. The Koreans had
protected them, and now they were bringing them in.

Native sleds were appearing. One was attached to the
rear of a jeep. Over a dozen men could be loaded in this
makeshift and driven ashore. Again the enemy would fire
at the jeep. Milton would duck his head, slew the sled
around, and drive madly for the trucks and tents on shore.

Chinese fire was growing. They were tossing in mortars
now. Beall called for armed support. Jeeploads of machine
gunners came out to mid-ice. They deployed around the
loading point. They began firing. The Chinese came down
to the ice in force. The Marine guns chattered, stopping
them. It was growing dark. Beall began to retire. The jeeps
and gunners leapfrogged backward, laying down a covering fire. An Army tank rolled into position below the ice
and raked the left side of the Reservoir to prevent the
Chinese from coming out to cut off Beall's men.

They got back safely—and they had rescued 319
wounded.

Almost all of these wounded men were immediately evacuated. Trucks bringing them to the hospital tents stopped only for evacuation tickets to be attached to the stiff and blood-caked clothing of their passengers. Then they rolled onto the airstrip to the rows of stretchers and the waiting airplanes. The wounded were carried aboard, flown out of Hagaru—moving in a few blurred hours from the cold dark night of their despair into the warmth and light of rear-area hospitals, the sound of American voices, and the touch of friendly, soothing hands cutting the wretched clothing off their torn and frozen bodies.

Thus did Beall and his Marines tear Task Force Faith's wounded out of the hands of the enemy and the cold. Nor did they cease with nightfall. In the following days, while the marching perimeters of the Fifth and Seventh were blasting their way south from Yudam-ni, they returned repeatedly to the rescue. Dozens more were saved.

Once an observation plane reported spotting four men out on the ice. Beall and Milton and Corporal William Howard drove to the Reservoir. They stopped their jeep at mid-ice and crawled to the first day's rescue area. They saw two men in a rowboat that had been frozen among the reeds of the enemy shore. Two others lay huddled about three hundred yards to the north, again inshore, and this time at the point where the Communists had massed for their attack.

It was a trap.

Beall toyed with the bait. He called to the men. No answer. Tentatively he and Milton and Howard crawled forward. Heavy machine-gun fire converged on them from three sides. They were pinned down.

Sweeping down from the skies in infuriated assault came two full squadrons of Marine fighters. The observation plane which had sighted the stricken men had called them down. Two full squadrons to rescue three Marines and four wounded soldiers—and they came in with a recklessness that roared the rage of those who rode their cockpits. They came in so low that they sucked the very snow off the ice. They came in not six feet above the surface, so close that Beall could think he might touch their underbellies with his BAR.

One plane made a pass. Its rockets streaked into the mouth of a cave where two heavy machine guns had been set up. Another flattened out and attacked. It obliterated another gun and its five-man crew directly to Beall's front. Rocketing, strafing, they broke the Chinese trap into pieces, and then shot the pieces into bits. And the last of the wounded were dragged to safety.

They were the last. Beall made sure of that. His final act was to approach the line of trucks standing silently on a road that ran to the right of the Reservoir, a bit above him. With the enemy fleeing the wrath falling from the skies, he was unmolested. He came to the stalled convoy. He slipped from truck to truck, peering inside, calling out. There were no answers.

Because there were no living.

CHAPTER FIFTEEN

————————

It was the end of the beginning. It was that day-light of December 2, during which Beall had commenced his ice rescue, through which Davis had perceived the friendly helmets of Fox Hill—and everywhere along The Road, those clenching fingers of General Sung Shin-lun were being broken, bent, or battered.

To the north the fighting columns of Litzenberg and Murray were bursting roadblocks, blasting south.

Below them Davis's battalion was clearing the last of the enemy from Toktong Pass.

Midway, at Hagaru, the aerial life line grew stronger and stronger. Now there were dozens of transports roaring in and out, bringing arms and men and food, taking out casualties by the hundreds.

Between Hagaru and Koto-ri, Marine air harried the Chinese on their ridges, and artillery from both towns converged in a rain of shells.

Between Koto and Chinhung-ni, a decisive reconnaissance rolled north.

On December 2, the Chinese tide was flowing to its term.

The Marines from Yudam-ni had fought their way down from the twin peaks.

While Davis's battalion had plunged into the trackless dark, the other battalions of Litzenberg and Murray had punched down The Road.

It was war by battalions. In that early-morning blackness of December 2, the rifle battalions were fighting everywhere, for the enemy was swarming everywhere—to the front, to the rear, on the flanks. Marines climbed mile-high mountains, and fought. They stumbled through jumbles of snow-filled scrubs, up draws, and across saddles, and fought. They withdrew, fighting. It was a fight for their own survival, and for the protection of the wounded and the regimental trains still crawling south as the fighting flared on, its enshrouded trucks and its guns glinting fitfully in the flashing and the thundering of the hills.

Then, a mile below the twin peaks, the column came to a halt. The Chinese held a heavy roadblock—they held it in strength under orders to hang on at all costs. The Third Battalion, Seventh, led by Lieutenant Colonel William Harris, went up against it. Three times this depleted battalion hurled itself upon the Chinese. Thrice they were thrown back. Just before dawn the Marines held only a slight penetration. Harris began to regroup. The enemy would certainly counterattack. He put Jig Company into line.

Today there is no "J" Company in the American infantry regiment. But Harris had one, another of those composites of necessity, and this was scornfully dubbed "Jig" because it was a jigsaw puzzle of cannoneers and headquarters oddments. In it were such men as James Johnson, an artillery sergeant turned rifleman for the breakout.

Jig Company went into line.

The counterattack came. It came with an overwhelming rush. It broke and routed almost all of Jig Company— all but that platoon which Sergeant Johnson took over when its leader fell dead. Johnson deployed his men in a skillful defense. They fought with valor. But they were not nearly enough to hold, and Johnson was ordered to withdraw. Erect, shouting above the battle, pointing carefully with his finger, the sergeant directed a man-by-man withdrawal. He faced the charging Chinese alone. He emptied his rifle and threw the last of his grenades. As daylight fingered the mountains, Johnson was locked in hand-to-hand combat with the enemy—and he was never seen again.

But Sergeant Johnson had gained time. The Chinese counterattack was shattered on the perimeter which had been building to his rear.

Now Darkhorse Battalion came into line. This was Lieutenant Colonel Robert Taplett's Third Battalion, Fifth, called "Darkhorse" after its radio signal call. Darkhorse was already less than half a battalion. The remnants had come down from high ground to the north, displacing under a devastating aerial and artillery barrage. They moved through Harris's men. They burst the roadblock, fighting down The Road in broad daylight. They would lead the way to Hagaru, battling for almost every foot of it, while that lone tank rumbled jauntily ahead, as though delighted by the charmed life it bore, its guns still barking defiance.

At midday on December 2, Darkhorse's How Company assaulted a towering mountain stronghold. It lay above the bend leading into Toktong Pass. Across its mile-high peak was the reinforced garrison of Fox Hill. How Com-

pany went up the height in the face of fierce small-arms
and automatic fire from its defenders. But by seven o'clock
at night they were dug in on its slopes.

On the other side of The Road, Item Company attacked
another height. These men also dug in, only to reel under
the savage blows aimed at them that night by counterattacking Chinese. They hung on desperately. Staff
Sergeant William Windrich fought to hold a vital position with a single squad. His men were cut to pieces.
Though hit in the head himself, Windrich ran through
the darkness to the rear, bringing men to help the wounded,
leading reinforcements to the position. He fought on. He
was shot in the legs. He stayed where he was. A Marine
crawled to him and sought to dress his wounds. Windrich
shoved him aside, gasping: "There isn't time. Besides,
they're only little holes." There was not much time—not
for Sergeant Windrich. In another hour his life had leaked
from those small holes—but his position had held. Item
Company had held all along its lines, though it now could
muster only 41 effectives of the 141 who had begun the
breakout the day before.

There were so many wounded now.

They were being brought down from the inflamed hillsides, laid in rows of stretchers beside The Road. Ambulances halted alongside them. Casualty trucks lurched to
a stop. Doctors and chaplains peered inside.

"Here, you're only shot in the shoulder. We need room
for this man. He's hit bad."

"Yes, sir."

"Frostbite? You can still stand, can't you?"

"Yes, sir."

They clambered down. Slowly, painfully, feeling the
first needles of returning circulation jabbing at numbed

flesh, in slings and bandages, faces pale from hunger and loss of blood, they got down and walked. They could not fight, but they could give up their place to a comrade who needed it, and there was always someone who needed it, somewhere down The Road.

And they were beginning to fall asleep as they walked.

Men who had lost the sensation of movement, who had felt the numbness rising slowly from their frozen feet, would suddenly slump, pitch into the snow. They would be seized, shaken, shouted at—kicked, if need be—and made to march on. They might plead to be left alone, but stronger, angry wills forced them forward. No one was left behind. Not even the dead. Their bodies were lashed to gun barrels, strapped to running boards, stretched across the hoods of trucks. They were dragged in sleds. They were brought out.

So the column moved, stuffed with wounded, laden with corpses, swept by sporadic gunfire, flanked by lines of woodenly marching men—halting here until a roadblock fell, there until bruised and broken wounded could be hauled up from a gully into which a casualty truck had plunged—but rolling steadily southward while the encompassing hills still crackled with the sound of battle.

On Fox Hill throughout the daylight of December 2, Captain Barber's men held the perimeter while Davis's battalion went over to the attack.

Davis's men were jaunty. They were already styling themselves "the Ridgerunners of Toktong Pass," and they were drawing strength from the knowledge that they had made that heroic march, though they would not call it that. They ate their icy clots of fruit and went in search of the enemy again, for the main body was approaching Toktong, and no Chinese could be left on high ground.

In a series of sharp fights, they cleared most of the Pass before nightfall. In one of these, Private James Beard fought with a verve and daring that characterized the new spirit animating his comrades. Beard wiped out half an enemy platoon with his BAR. He charged one position after another, throwing grenades to flush the enemy into the open, firing at them from the hip as he closed. His foray ended when his ammunition ran out.

But at nightfall there were still Chinese in the Toktong area, perhaps a battalion of them. The men on Fox Hill deliberately built fires, tempting the enemy to shoot and reveal their positions. The foe fell for this ancient ruse. They opened up. Flashes were marked in a valley. Knowing then where the Chinese were, the Ridgerunners of Toktong Pass went out after them.

What they did not know was that behind the hill overlooking the valley lay most of the Darkhorse Battalion.

The plane had no business being there on the airstrip at Hagaru, but it was welcome. When it had dropped below the overcast and skimmed the ridges surrounding the airfields, everyone had pointed at it and shouted in mixed dismay and delight.

"Fer Gawd's sake, it's a four-engine job!"

"He ain't gonna make it. He ain't gonna land no R5D on this goddam postage stamp!"

But he did. With monumental disdain for those theories setting 4,000 feet as minimum landing space for his Skymaster, with good-natured scorn for the crash crews hastily gathering on the airstrip rim, Navy Chief B. J.

Miller brought his four-engine craft safely down on
Hagaru's 2,900 feet of prepared surface.

The Marines stifled their exclamations of astonishment
and quickly loaded thirty-nine wounded aboard Miller's
plane. Then the big craft taxied to the rough end of the
strip. It swung around. It rolled forward, bumping, its
wings teetering and flopping. It hit the prepared surface
with a roar of gunned motors and drove upward in a sharp
climb. It cleared the first line of ridges by a few dozen feet,
and then it was safely airborne. Looking down at tiny
Hagaru, with its tents, its headquarters bungalow, its
black dots in the snow marking the Marine trenches, Miller
and his gallant crewmen let out their breaths and laughed.
That would show those crazy Jarheads . . . Next time they
were on liberty and met one of them sounding off about
Frozen Chosin . . .

In his bungalow, Major General Oliver P. Smith was
unaware of this unorthodox contribution of the Navy to
the support of Hagaru. But his reports did tell him that
this second day of evacuation would see some nine hundred
casualties air-lifted to safety. Other reports told him that
Fox Hill had been relieved and that Litzenberg and
Murray were breaking out. Though they were taking
heavy casualties, they were confident they could make it.
They hoped to gain Hagaru by nightfall tomorrow,
December 3.

If they did, and General Smith never doubted that they
would, the critical point would have been passed. What
remained?

The Road to the south.

There was no doubt that once the First Marine Division
regrouped at Hagaru and struck south again, it would

encounter heavy opposition en route to Koto. But that
was a matter of men and arms. That would be done.

But between Koto and Chinhung-ni lay two great barriers.

The first was a water-gate bridge three and a half miles
below Koto. Here water from Chosin Reservoir fell from
a tunnel into four penstocks, or large steel pipes. These
ran sharply down the mountainside, bringing the water
to a power plant in the valley below. On the uphill side the
pipes were covered by a concrete gatehouse having no floor.
On the other was this vital one-way bridge. It spanned the
pipes, which lay some twenty feet below it, and beneath
them, a narrow abyss plunging a thousand feet or so to
a jumble of rocks. If the bridge were destroyed, there
would be no hope of by-pass for the vehicles. It would
simply have to be rebuilt. As Smith knew, it had already
been blown twice and had been twice restored. This meant
that it could be destroyed again, and the Chinese held the
twelve miles of road between Koto and Chinhung. They
could blow the bridge whenever they wished. They probably would, Smith thought, and yet there was nothing to
do but have it watched. Meantime he would get Partridge
working on a plan to meet that eventuality.

The second barrier was Funchilin Pass. It lay about
three miles below the bridge, receiving The Road as it ran
eastward and turning it sharply south again. Commanding Funchilin Pass was a steep mountain peak which was
marked on Smith's map as Hill 1081. This the Chinese
held in strength. They had been reinforcing it since they
had seized The Road between Koto and Chinhung on the
night of November 29.

General Smith had to have Funchilin Pass.

And he had the force that could take it. Lieutenant

Colonel Donald Schmuck's First Battalion, First, was emplaced in Chinhung. Schmuck could march north and seize Hill 1081. His action could remove the last barrier between safety and the sea, once the Division had broken out of Koto and crossed the bridge. Yet, Smith thought, it would be foolish to attempt it now. It would be premature. It would tip his hand. Its seizure should be timed to coincide with breakout from Koto. That would be another week or so. Still, Hill 1081 should be reconnoitered now.

General Smith called upon Schmuck to make his reconnaissance.

The commander of the First Battalion, First, had long since realized the importance of that hill mass up The Road. He had expected to be ordered to seize it. He was not surprised to be instructed to scout it.

On that morning of December 2, he got his scouting party ready.

First, he formed a decoy. He sent a platoon of riflemen up the valley along the railroad track. They were instructed to make their movement obvious, to deploy in view of the enemy. They did.

An hour later, Schmuck's sneak patrol set out. There was about a squad of men in three jeeps and a small truck. They included an artillery observer, with radio, and Schmuck himself was the over-all commander.

They rolled up The Road unobserved. They drove about five miles. Then, a mile or so short of Hill 1081, they stopped and dismounted. They turned the vehicles around, facing south. They left a guard behind and moved out on foot, keeping to the snow-covered ridge slopes. They moved around a bend. They stopped in astonishment.

There, stretching as far as their eyes could see, covering the hillside like a colony of cliff dwellers, was a numerous, nonchalant enemy.

They were there in swarms. They were cooking, shaking out blankets, chatting, dragging brush through the snow for warmth, digging bunkers, reinforcing holes—doing everything that troops do in broad daylight when there is no foe for miles around. If they looked anywhere, they looked north. That was where the American Marines were.

Schmuck decided to get a closer look. The patrol moved around a few more bends. They stopped by the roadside. They saw more of the enemy, still unconcerned, still busy at the humdrum of daily life on a quiet front.

It was child's play for Schmuck to plot their positions on the aerial maps which he had received a few days before. He sent his artillery observer and a few others up a hill to the right, and stayed beside The Road, pondering.

He had never before been presented such an opportunity. He would probably finish his career without another to match it. He made up his mind. He called for artillery fire.

The observer contacted the guns back in Koto. Schmuck gave him the order. The shells came whistling down upon those hills. They came in accurately. They arrived in volume. Atop his hill, the observer guided them to targets unobserved by Schmuck.

It was a slaughter.

In one instant, beguiling confidence—in the next, pure terror tearing at the innards of those devastated Chinese. They scuttled over their hillsides in a panic. That sudden rain of shells snapped their wills and made their hearts flabby with fear, as happens to all men when the scythe of death sweeps among them on an instant and invisibly.

They bowlegged it wildly to their holes or threw themselves in the snow or rolled down the slopes.

Lieutenant Colonel Schmuck permitted himself perhaps a minute of satisfied observation before recalling the hilltop party and racing down The Road to the vehicles. They made them in good order. Seeing them coming, hearing the outgoing barrage, the drivers had jumped behind the wheels and had the motors running.

"Take off!" Schmuck shouted, and then, to no one in particular, as the jeeps leaped forward and went lurching down The Road: "Damned if that wasn't the most beautiful sight I've seen since I came to Korea!"

If it had been, he had been wise not to tarry to behold it. For shots broke out behind them. A party of Chinese was rounding the bend to the north, moving along the railroad tracks. In a few more seconds the patrol had skidded around a curve and out of the Chinese riflemen's sight.

They had just got away.

Farther down The Road, Schmuck pulled his decoy patrol in behind him and the entire group gained Chinhung within another fifteen minutes. They had struck the enemy a savage blow and had not suffered a scratch. Better than that, Schmuck now knew the Chinese positions. Nor could they be altered, unless the enemy was willing to surrender the advantage of terrain.

In another week, when Schmuck marched his Marines north under cover of a howling blizzard, they would know exactly where to strike.

CHAPTER SIXTEEN

DAWN of December 3 was breaking between Yudam-ni and Fox Hill, and with it a shout was breaking from the throat of Colonel Homer Litzenberg. It was unlike Litzenberg to shout, but he was yelling as he turned from his radio to Lieutenant Colonel Murray, his comrade of the council of war.

"Ray! Ray! Tell Taplett that the Chinese are running into his arms!"

They were. They were blundering into a trap set by coincidence and circumstance. The Ridgerunners who had gone after them during the night were now driving them downhill into the guns of Darkhorse Battalion. And neither one knew that the other was there.

But Murray was quickly informing Taplett of the opportunity. Taplett called for artillery. Not getting it, he called for an air strike. A pair of Corsairs dropped cautiously out of the overcast. They made their approach.

And then the overcast lifted, revealing almost an entire battalion of enemy retreating down the side of that mile-high mountain from which the Ridgerunners had dislodged them. Taplett's heavy machine guns and rifles and

mortars opened up. The Corsairs struck with rockets and
Napalm. The Ridgerunners joined the shooting. Every
weapon that the planes and the two Marine battalions could
use was fired at the demoralized enemy. At half past ten in
the morning, when only desultory rifle shots rang out in
the frozen hills, when the butchery was done, Taplett
reported to Murray that the Chinese battalion had been
"completely eliminated."

So, too, was eliminated the last concerted attempt to
deny Toktong Pass to the Marines. It was now a matter of
mopping up. By one o'clock Davis's men held all the hills,
and they were standing on them expectantly, gazing anxiously up The Road.

Far below them they saw a tiny buglike shape poking its
snout around a bend. It crawled into full view, dark against
the snow. It was that leading tank.

"It's them!" the Ridgerunners shouted. "They're here,
they're here!"

Then gradually appeared all of that column, the trucks,
the jeeps, the ambulances, the towed guns with barrels
throwing oddly thickened silhouettes against the sky, bearing burdens which those silently watching Ridgerunners
could comprehend—and count more glorious than grisly—
the lines of marching men, the flanking companies deploying through the snow, and above it all the warplanes
darting and swooping. They saw the column from on high,
saw it dwarfed into insignificance by that height. And yet
they could feel its grandeur swelling their own hearts, they
could know that the hot tears were not entirely of the cold
wind wailing about them.

The column was moving through Toktong Pass. The
vital junction was being made, the basic maneuver of
breakout from Yudam-ni was being completed. Now, it

remained for the men of Darkhorse to fight the remaining six miles south to Hagaru, for the Ridgerunners to descend and move in behind them, for the dead and wounded of Fox Hill to be carried down to The Road, and for the 80 effectives of Captain Barber's original force of 240 men to depart their hill, erect and undefeated.

The last of the wounded to be carried down was Private Hector Cafferata. He had lain on his stretcher while Fox Hill was being swept bare. Only the frozen bodies of the enemy would be left to greet the darkness of another night. Tents were struck and bundled off. All superfluous gear was burned. All else was lugged down to the regimental trains—stoves, mortars, water cans, radios, rations, even the sheets of parachute silk. Cafferata had heard these sounds of evacuation, had watched his comrades stagger past him with their loads. He had seen the wounded borne out of sight, one by one, until at last he was alone. He wondered. He did not doubt, he wondered only if perhaps he were not so badly hurt. For here he was, the last to go . . .

Then he heard the crunch of many footsteps in the snow. He heard the rasping voice of the sergeant whose arm he had so solicitously sought to break, fortunately failing, for the sergeant would win a Silver Star for his work on Fox Hill.

"Awright, yuh big ape," the voice growled. "I suppose yuh was feelin' sorry for yerself. Figgered we'd leave yuh."

Cafferata gasped an unintelligible insult, and Sergeant Dee-Jay laughed.

"Yuh oughta know we'd need a goddam squad to lug yuh down the hill, yuh big goon. It just took a while roundin' up volunteers."

So they bore him down, eight of them, for Cafferata was

still a giant and the face of Fox Hill was steep. They brought him to The Road and laid him atop a tarpaulin on a truck. And then, as the truck pulled away, Cafferata at last succumbed to the temptation that had plucked at him throughout six days and nights in the casualty tent.

He pulled the tarpaulin over his face and closed his eyes.

A less than blessed dark enshrouded the eyes of the four Marines who still lived in that wretched roadside hut of Hell-Fire Valley. It was the fourth night since the ambush of Task Force Drysdale, when they had been left to perish by their Chinese captors. They had lived, hardly conscious that they lived, drifting through a dim twilight of regained consciousness, as though afloat on a dark cold sea of pain and half-remembered forms, plunging again into the oblivion of sleep. Sometimes, at night, they could hear movement and voices whispering a foreign tongue. It would be the Korean villagers coming again. They came at night, for they feared to show themselves by day. They brought water to the lips of the suffering, gave them their own crude gruel to eat, adjusted the stiff blankets that covered them. They could bring no medicine, for they had none. But they brought themselves and the hope contained in the eagerness of those voices hissing "American . . . GI . . . come . . ." They knew that the Marines were fighting into Hagaru from Yudam-ni. They could guess that they would come still farther down The Road to the hut. So they brought the water and the food and the pitiful small warmth, and also that better thing, almost equal to life itself, which was their hope.

The Ridgerunners were taking prisoners. Patrols probing the hills to the flanks were coming upon parties of

Chinese who no longer wished to fight. They had thrown away their weapons. They had huddled together in holes and crevices. They were starving, near frozen, an enemy no longer to be feared but only pitied. The hardship of the hills had been too great for these peasant soldiers who had been reared in privation and trained to endure. Whatever it was that had sustained these Marines—leadership, training, better equipment or superior communciation, esprit, steadier will—whatever it was, these Chinese did not possess. Those who were not already frozen dead or beyond help were led down to the column.

The point of the column was nearing Hagaru. It was close to seven o'clock on the night of December 3. Many more hours would be required before the tail of the column at last dragged into Hagaru, and, during them, there occurred one of those moments of panic which always seem to precede triumph.

Eight prime movers towing 155mm howitzers had run out of Diesel fuel. They were stalled, awaiting oil to be rushed to them from the point where it had been air-dropped. In that interval a gap appeared. In that interval the Chinese blew a small bridge over a frozen stream and built up a covering fire.

Trucks began to pile up while the engineers worked frantically to repair the break. Two truck drivers were killed. Some of the others gave way to panic. They tried to dash across the ice to safety. Confusion was mounting. Discipline was disappearing. The iron order that had brought the column through could be shattered into fragments.

A truck towing a 105mm howitzer skidded around in full and rabbity retreat. It was immediately pursued by Chief Warrant Officer Allen Carlson and a stream of splendid vituperation unrivaled even in the hearing of these Marines. Carlson sent the Verb thundering through those hills, that Verb, that single, ugly, four-letter word that lies embedded like a dirty, recurrent jewel in the mosaic of Marine profanity. He applied the Verb to the driver, to his ancestors, to his truck and his howitzer, and repeatedly to his retreating backside. Carlson disappeared around a bend in the road. He reappeared, leading a shaken driver and howitzer to the roadblock. He set it up and blasted point-blank at the enemy position. A 75mm recoilless rifle barked angrily. Another howitzer gave voice, joined by a heavy machine gun. A rifle platoon attacked. The roadblock fell at the expense of 150 Chinese dead.

The Verb had conquered, as it often does, and the column moved on.

The short, white-coated shapes flitted softly down the hills between Koto and Chinhung. Some carried rifles and automatic weapons. Others had their weapons slung, and their shadows were made sharp by the cases of explosive that they carried. They came to the bridge which spanned the chasm in which the water pipes lay. A group of them went across, their passage obscured by the looming bulk of the gatehouse, and then they reappeared above it, deploying, setting up their weapons.

The others busied themselves under the bridge. They worked clumsily, they, too, complaining with soft bitterness of the cold that made blundering sticks of their fingers. At last it was ready. The covering patrol was called back. All retreated behind a ridge fold and lay down.

A roar and a flash shook and lighted the hills. Falling fragments of metal clanged on The Road or plopped into the snow.

A lone figure, an officer, stole silently up to the chasm. He peered over. Nothing. He returned to his men, elated. The bridge was blown.

At Hagaru the British Royal Marines and a platoon of tanks had gone out to clear The Road north of the perimeter, to lay down covering fire for the column now approaching. Word spread rapidly among Hagaru's defenders that the column was coming down from Yudam-ni. Crowds of Marines began gathering north of the town, anxiously watching, silent . . .

A convoy of trucks rolled darkly into view. They halted about five hundred yards above the perimeter. Wounded and frostbitten Marines clambered down. Shadowy shapes moved up behind them, platoons of riflemen. They closed. They formed ranks. They began to walk. Slowly, painfully, heads rose and shoulders straightened. Shoe-pacs fell with soft irregular sounds on that frozen road. A cadence grew. Now the muffled footfalls came in precision. A marching rhythm swept those ragged ranks. Eyes sunken in haggard, bearded faces stared straight ahead.

They came marching in.

CHAPTER SEVENTEEN

AT TWO o'clock in the afternoon of December 4, the last of the men from Yudam-ni had gained Hagaru. It had taken 59 hours for the point to march those 14 miles, 79 for the tail. Litzenberg and Murray had come in with some 1,500 casualties, although perhaps a third of these were nonbattle, chiefly frostbite.

Many of the frostbitten, the lightly wounded would be treated and returned to action. A new and severe standard of evacuation had been adopted, had already reduced the outflow from some nine hundred on December 2 to seven hundred on December 3. Captain Bud Hering, the division's senior medical officer, had discovered that the Air Force officer on the strip had not been screening the evacuees. He had said it was not his responsibility, which it was not. Hering shouldered this unpleasant task. His standard was related to the condition of Lieutenant Commander Chester Lessenden, the Fifth's regimental surgeon. Lessenden, with two painfully frozen feet, had refused evacuation.

Personally passing on each borderline case, Hering

cleared those who were as bad as Lessenden, rejected those
who were better.

Even so, 1,000 casualties would be evacuated from
Hagaru on December 4.

But the First Marine Division still had plenty left.
Having suffered a total of 2,260 battle casualties since
November 27—plus 1,072 nonbattle casualties—there remained around 17,000 men along The Road from Hagaru
to Koto to Chinhung.

In Hagaru, General Smith commanded some 10,000
troops, of which all but about 1,500 were men of his First
Division. The other 1,500 consisted of Tenth Corps head-
quarters troops, a few ROK police, 125 British Royal
Marines, and a provisional battalion of 385 survivors of
Task Force Faith under the command of Lieutenant
Colonel Norman Anderson.

Enemy casualties had been staggering, probably five
or six times those of the Marines. Upward of 15,000
Chinese had been lost since November 27, and the three
divisions which General Sung had employed in the north—
the 59th, 79th, and 89th—were out of the fight. There
were no figures on General Sung's non-battle casualties,
though captured Communist documents would show some
units made ineffectual by frostbite casualties as high as
80 per cent. But General Sung still had 40,000 men—the
58th, 60th, 77th, and 78th Divisions—in the hills commanding the 21 miles of road between Hagaru and Chinhung-ni. The Chinese had been steadily reinforcing, and
as General Smith knew by that afternoon of December 4,
the vital water-gate bridge beneath Koto had been blown.

But Smith had been prepared for this. He ordered an
aerial reconnaissance of the bridge site, and notified

Lieutenant Colonel Partridge to stand by for conferences on the subject.

Next, General Smith began to write an order for the destruction of $13,000 worth of Post Exchange supplies that had been trucked to Hagaru in the early, Home-for-Christmas days. Now of course, they were useless. But, no! The stores included cases of Tootsie Rolls and Charms candy. They wouldn't freeze, they could be issued for rations. General Smith revised his order, excluding the candy from it. The Marines would come marching out of Hagaru sucking Tootsie Rolls and Charms, while more than one truck would have its leaking radiator plugged with wads of chewing gum.

Next, there was the curious complaint of the Air Force Cargo Command. They were running short of parachutes for their air drops. Where were they? The troops had them. They used them for blankets. With wry reluctance, Smith ordered them recovered. After all, the men would be soon marching again. Some one hundred tons of parachutes were flown out of Hagaru.

There was also a gentle reproach from Tenth Corps. It had been found that the Marines were flying out their dead, as well as wounded. Oliver Smith received and filed the rebuke. He knew that living Marines had risked death to rescue the bodies of their buddies. The dead would continue to be flown out.

There was the problem of regroupment at Hagaru, of re-forming for the fresh attack toward Koto-ri. Smith would have liked to press on with all possible speed. He was loathe to delay and let the enemy build up his forces. But the men who had broken out of Yudam-ni needed a rest. Their wounded had to be got out. Yet they could not wait past December 6. And so he ordered a staff already badly riddled by enemy bullets to commence planning for the breakout, giving them two days to master a logistical problem of setting a fighting column of a thousand vehicles and ten thousand men into motion. Moreover they must devise ways of getting rid of excess equipment. Smith was leaving the enemy nothing. Not a jeep, not a rifle, not a can of beans.

And what of the great supplies of artillery shells piling up in Hagaru? Simple. Fire them at the enemy before they jumped off.

Again, supporting air had to be reminded to continue the interdiction of all buildings within five miles to either side of The Road.

And Oliver Smith himself had to be reminded that General Almond would be arriving soon, bringing Distinguished Service Crosses for Litzenberg and Murray, for Beall—and for him.

There were the Marine replacements being flown into Hagaru, mostly men returned to duty from the hospitals. Some of them had arrived. In all, 537 would come in. General Smith assigned them to Lieutenant Colonel Ridge, the commander of Hagaru's perimeter who was resuming command of his Third Battalion, First. They were forming now, outside Smith's headquarters.

General Smith stepped outside to clear his lungs of the bungalow's foul air. He saw a young Marine squatting dejectedly in the snow, awaiting his turn to plod off to Ridge's unit. He approached him.

"What's the matter, son?"

"They're putting me in the Third Batt, First, sir."

"Yes?"

"But that ain't my outfit, sir. I belong to Second Batt."

General Smith smiled. "You're in the Third Batt, now, son," he said gently. "Maybe when we get to Koto you can go back to your old outfit."

The Marine tried to smile. "Well, if you say so, sir, I guess that's it."

That was it, and General Smith returned to his bungalow to stand beneath the photograph of Joseph Stalin to think out his solution to one last, insignificant problem that irritated him beyond measure.

War correspondents had been coming into Hagaru since the airfield went into service. Generally they flew in by day, departing the same night. They had been filing stories studded with such irksome words as "trap" and "retreat." For the first time in history, it was reported, United States Marines were retreating. But General Smith had never considered his division to be trapped, nor was he pleased to see "retreat" used to describe the operation he was conducting. Immensely proud of a difficult campaign that actually was proceeding "according to plan," General Smith decided to meet with the newsmen.

Very carefully, he began to define the military meaning of the word "retreat." It was, he said, an orderly retirement to the rear forced upon you by the enemy. It implied that your forces held the ground to the rear. But here, he continued, the enemy held the ground to the front *and* the rear. And the destruction of this enemy remained the purpose of the First Marine Division.

"So you see, gentlemen," he concluded mildly, "we are not retreating. We are merely attacking in another direction."

They pounced upon this definition with delight. It went out to the world, prefixed by a very un-Smithian "Retreat, hell!" It went into American history, beside General

McAuliffe's "Nuts!" at Bastogne, Dewey's "Damn the
torpedoes!" at Manila Bay and that "Retreat, hell—we
just got here!" uttered by another Marine officer in
Belleau Wood. It became immortal.

H-E-L-P

The pilot of the observation plane could read the letters
plainly. They had been stamped into the snow in hills
lying to the east of The Road—that is, to the left going
down it. The pilot let his craft down and came in low. He
saw a half-dozen figures running through the snow, waving
wildly at him. He waved back, and headed for Koto-ri.

In a half-hour he was back. He dropped food and
medical supplies and a message saying that help would be
forthcoming. Then the pilot flew away, happy to have
come to the aid of a party of brother Leathernecks.

But these were British Royal Marines, twenty-two
survivors of Task Force Drysdale who had been cut off
and had been holing up in the hills for five days.

Daylight of December 4 was fading into dusk, but they
were still flying casualties out of Hagaru. A young Marine
was brought into an airfield aid station. He had a badly
mangled foot. A doctor approached him, and the youth
said: "Don't try to kid me, Doc, I know the foot is gone.
But I want to ask one question." The doctor paused,
lighted a cigarette, passed it to him, and said: "What's
your question?" The Marine took a preliminary puff,
tried to grin, and replied: "If they give me an artifical
foot, can I still dance on it?"

The night of December 4 was again quiet at Hagaru,
while the planners of Major General Smith's depleted

staff worked on. Their plan would be ready by the following morning. It called for breakout to Koto-ri, still held
by Puller, and followed the same tactics that had brought
the men down from Yudam-ni.

To the Fifth Regiment fell the vital task of clearing
the enemy from that troublesome East Hill. For this height
commanded The Road down which the Seventh would be
attacking. Once this was done, the Fifth would fall in as
the tail.

Again, no one would ride but casualties, drivers, and
some radio operators. Everyone else would walk. Two days'
rations would be taken. Groups of trucks were placed under
individual commanders, with orders to deploy in covered-
wagon style should the column be halted. Stalled trucks
would be pushed to the side of The Road, destroyed if they
could not be repaired. Except for the lone tank in the
point, tanks would bring up the rear, for they could block
passage if immobilized.

Massive air support was planned. One of the greatest
concentrations of air power since the Korean War began
would hammer the Chinese forces which General Sung
was rushing south. Naval pilots from the carriers *Leyte*,
Valley Forge, *Philippine Sea*, and *Princeton* would join
Marine fliers from Yonpo and the carrier *Baedong Strait*.
The Fifth Air Force would add United States and Australian fighter-bombers to this close-up interdiction, while
heavier bombers would deliver long-range attacks on the
enemy. With the coming of darkness Marine night hecklers
would be on station.

Operation orders for this plan were issued at eight
o'clock on the morning of December 5. Jump-off time was
set for first light the next day.

During the intervening day, aerial evacuation was

stepped up to a rate of 1,400 casualties. Another 60 would be flown out the next day, before Hagaru was abandoned, making a final total of 4,312 wounded and disabled removed to hospitals from the tiny airfield that had been whittled out of that frozen earth. And the bodies of 137 Marines had also been taken out.

It was a triumph of foresight and engineering ingenuity. It was as satisfying to Major General William Tunner, chief of the Air Force Combat Cargo Command, as it was to Major General Smith. For General Tunner flew into Hagaru on that intervening day of December 5 to suggest that aerial evacuation might solve the entire division's problem.

"I've got plenty of planes, Smith," he said. "When we get all the wounded out, we can start flying your division out."

Smith shook his head. He said nothing of the difficulties attendant on such a maneuver, of what might happen to a gradually diminishing rearguard holding a perimeter against a gradually increasing enemy.

"No able-bodied man flies out of here," he replied. "I've been flying them in. We're fighting our way out."

Such was the spirit now taking hold of the force at Hagaru, and so it was being expressed by the Marines themselves. Lieutenant Colonel Murray had gathered his commanders to inform them of the Fifth's new mission at East Hill. He said:

"We'll hold our present positions until the Seventh clears the road to Koto, after which we'll move out. When we do move out, we will come out as Marines and not as stragglers. We're going to take our dead, wounded, and equipment when we leave. We're coming out, I tell you, as Marines—or not at all. Any officer who doesn't think that we can get out of here will kindly get **frostbite** and go lame and I'll see that he's evacuated."

Thus the lull of the last full day at Hagaru. Then the last night—a dark flashing with the guns of the Eleventh Marines "expending" surplus ammunition on the enemy to the south.

Tomorrow, at six o'clock, they would be **attacking**.

In another direction.

CHAPTER EIGHTEEN

IT WAS six o'clock on the morning of December 6, and the remnant of Fox Hill was attacking.

They had been attached to Lieutenant Colonel Davis's Ridgerunners, these 80 survivors of the stand at Toktong, and now they were in the column point. They skirmished in staggered lines to either side of The Road, advancing behind the leading tank, advancing in a light fog and through a rain of bullets that not even Hagaru's thundering artillery could silence.

Bullets plunged down from the slopes, swept in from the flanks. Bullets whispered overhead, spanged off the ground with sharp wailing sounds, plucked at clothing, lodged in flesh. Men were falling, but the cry "Keep moving, keep moving!" spurred the others onward. They couldn't halt. They had the point, and the regimental trains were impatient to move out.

Pfc. Kenneth Benson was close behind the tank. He could envy his buddies, Cafferata, the others, Captain Barber. *They* had had it. Wounded though they might be, they were at least lying in hospital beds in Japan.

But *he* still had a long way to go. He and the others and gravel-voiced Sergeant Dee-Jay.

"Keep moving!" Dee-Jay yelled, and they scampered forward. Sometimes they leaped into the roadside ditches when the tank took a Chinese position under fire. Then they'd chomp their teeth on the lumps of Tootsie Roll softening in their mouths, eagerly gulping the juice. Sometimes Benson lay face upward, watching the tank, conscious of the carton of Post Exchange chewing gum in his pack, hard and flat against his back. But, always, "Keep moving!" and they'd be up and stumbling forward again.

At seven o'clock they had gone perhaps a mile of the eleven miles to Koto-ri. The tank rumbled around a bend. They followed. Gunfire came from a house to the left of The Road. Bullets clanged off the tank's steel hide. Benson jumped into a ditch. The tank swung around and rolled to a halt above him. He could see its 90mm rifle swiveling on target. It roared and flashed flame.

Benson felt himself raised into the air and slammed back against the rocklike earth. Behind him in the ditch, Dee-Jay called: "Did he get it?"

"He missed," Benson gasped. "An' I'm getting the hell outta here!"

He hunched erect and scrambled up the ditch. A savage blow struck his left shoulder and knocked him sprawling. He had hunched too high. A Chinese machine-gun bullet had pierced the knob of the shoulder and come out his back. It shredded his pack and made a hot paste in the center of the chewing gum. Falling, Benson heard the tank's cannon roar again. There was an explosion to his left, followed by the cheers of the Marines. The tank had knocked out the enemy position.

But the enemy had knocked Benson out of the war.

Sergeant Dee-Jay was beside him.

"Son of a bitch, they got yuh good! Lookit yer pack!"

The sergeant fashioned a sling out of Benson's cartridge bandoleer, talking to him meanwhile: "Lookit, Bens —yuh can either try to make it walking the rest of the way or try to catch one of the last planes outta Hagaru. Whatta ya say?"

"I'll try the plane," Benson muttered.

"Okay, g'wan back, then. An' listen, how about loanin' me that little pistol I sold yuh? I mean, it ain't no good to yuh now."

Benson grinned weakly. His right hand dived beneath his parka, unbuckled his belt and slid the holster and pistol free. He handed it over.

"Thanks, Bens—I'll pay yuh for it when I see yuh." There was a pause. "If I see yuh." The sergeant patted the private gently on the arm. "So long, kid. I hope yuh catch the plane." Then he was gone, running low down The Road, shouting again and again, "Keep moving! Keep moving!"

Benson lurched out of the ditch. He turned his face toward Hagaru and began to walk. His left shoulder and arm were already numbed and useless. And yet, he felt sheepish, walking back to Hagaru. He tried to avoid the eyes of the Ridgerunners coming down. He could guess what they were thinking. Now, *he* had had it. And *they* had a long way to go.

One of them growled, "Lucky bastard," and Benson tried to grin as he muttered, "Yeah, Semper Fi, boys—I got mine, how'd you make out?"

He trudged on, conscious of neither feet nor shoulder nor arm. He regained Hagaru by midmorning. He made

the airfield a half-hour later. He had his wound dressed
and was ticketed for evacuation—on the last plane leaving
Hagaru. He climbed aboard. He was made uneasy by
the sight of holes in the plane's fuselage. Then they were
taking off, straining aloft with a roar of gunned motors.
Below him he could see guns flashing in the hills. He held
his breath. The Chinese were still shooting at him.

But they were not. The guns Pfc. Benson had seen as
he left the war forever were those of the Second Battalion,
Fifth, hammering the main enemy positions on East Hill.

Lieutenant Colonel Roise's Second Battalion had struck
at East Hill almost simultaneously with the jump-off
south to Koto-ri. They had swept with astonishing ease
through the sector to which the Chinese had been clinging tenaciously for eight days. They routed them, killing
30, at the cost of one Marine killed and three wounded.
Success followed success when another ridge was taken
commanding The Road south. The Chinese seemed to be
collapsing. Then, in late afternoon, they were observed
massing for a counterattack on this ridge. Marine air was
called down on them. Two of Roise's companies delivered
a withering fire into their midst. Caught in these interlocking fires, the counterassault fell apart, and the Chinese
began surrendering by the score. A single Marine platoon
rounded up 220 captives. Now the Marines would not
only march out with their own dead and wounded, they
would bring their prisoners with them as well.

With the advent of dusk, the fighting at East Hill
seemed to be over. The Second Battalion's two companies,
augmented by an antitank squad and a platoon from the
Army's Fourth Signal Battalion, were confidently digging
in. So was a company of Ridge's Third Battalion, First,
and another from the First Battalion, Fifth.

With dark came the most ferocious, the most fatalistic, the most futile onslaught of all that Chosin Reservoir campaign. Some day, the world may know (if it should really care) what led that Chinese Communist commander to send thousands of soldiers shuffling through the snow to massacre. Did he think to retake East Hill, skillfully defended as it was in strength and backed by every variety of supporting arms? Did he prefer death, his own destruction multiplied by hundreds, to a report of failure? Was it to be a holocaust offered on the altar of the new China, with the phoenix of glory rising from the ashes of defeat? Or was it born of despair, that unbridled fury which has changed so many battles? Whatever the reason for it, it came—it came after dark with gradually mounting savagery. Thrice, four times, the white-quilted soldiers materialized out of the night, their coming heralded by their bugle calls and whistles, and each time they were riddled and slashed and heaped in the snow without so much as having gained grenade range. And after midnight they came no longer in waves—they came in an uninterrupted flow, the harsh whiteness of the illumination shells lighting the regular columns trotting forward, almost submissively forward, almost without hint of ardor, and deploying to their death among the bullets, among the tank and artillery shells, the mortars and rockets thundering and crashing in a most awful requiem for that charge. Sometimes they reached grenade-throwing range, and sometimes Marines died or were wounded. But the last struggle for East Hill was not a struggle at all. It was a simple slaughter. Holocaust it was, and for the new China there can be little comfort of glory rising from a field on which as many as 1,200 Chinese lay slain, from which the wounded were fleeing in hundreds, writing in the white snow the red legends of that utter defeat.

By morning there was no longer any doubt about East Hill. The Corsairs were back on station, scattering the enemy. Murray had already ordered two of his battalions, as well as Ridge's battalion, to begin displacing downhill to the south and Koto. With daybreak only Roise's battalion, a platoon of tanks, and groups of demolition men from the engineers would be in Hagaru.

Before they left, they would give the deathblow to that unfortunate dying hill town.

Major General Oliver P. Smith had also arisen with first light on the morning of December 6. It was his custom to sleep through the night, awakening at dawn. Colonel Gregon Williams, his chief of staff, stood the night watch, bedding down in a truck sometime in midmorning. Now at work beneath that photograph of Joseph Stalin for the last time, General Smith saw with satisfaction that the fog had lifted, that Marine air was at work, and he received the reports of success from Litzenberg to the south, Murray to the east.

They would make Koto.

Now for the first barrier—the blown bridge—between Koto and Chinhung. General Smith summoned Lientenant Colonel Partridge. They discussed the results of the aerial reconnaissance on December 4. They decided that a Bailey bridge would not serve their purpose. A Treadway bridge, not so wide, seemed more likely. They telephoned Koto and found to their pleasure that Colonel Hugh McGraw's 185th Army Engineering Battalion there included the 58th Treadway Bridge Company among its units. But

they had no steel bridge sections. Smith decided to send
Partridge on a personal aerial reconnaissance. But before
he left, Smith began to question him about alternatives—
air shipments of precut lumber, the trial air-dropping of
the sections to make certain they could be delivered un-
damaged, the necessity of dropping enough sections for
two bridges, in case some were captured by the enemy.
Smith pressed his engineering officer for some minutes, de-
termined to turn every corner beforehand. At last, exasperated, the normally laconic Partridge exploded:

"Dammit, sir! I got you across the Han River at Seoul
and I got you an airfield at Hagaru—and I'll get you a
goddam bridge at Koto!"

In another minute, Partridge departed, mortified. But
Smith chuckled to himself. His engineering officer, so long
reserved and hesitant, was now displaying the aplomb of
the Old Breed.

He could swear at the commanding general.

South of Hagaru, the head of the column was slugging
slowly downroad. They had blasted through the first of
nine roadblocks the Chinese had thrown across The Road
between Hagaru and Koto-ri. Companies of riflemen were
leapfrogging one another, sometimes without meeting
serious opposition, sometimes running into heavy fire.

Fox Company was still on the left. The men moved
along a stream bed. It was frozen, like the icicles depend-
ing from their stubbles of beard, like the wind-made tears
on their cheeks, like their feet dragging through a foot
of new snow, the hands that grasped weapons without feeling them.

Machine guns on the left opened up. A Marine sank
silently to the ice. Mortars crashed among them, flinging

plumes of snow into the air. The Marines scattered along the stream bed, throwing themselves down on the ice. They ducked behind the shield formed by the shallow leftward bank. They opened fire on the enemy strong point very close to The Road. But they were too low. They were firing over the enemy's head. They were pinned down. They began calling frantically.

"Air! Where the hell's the air?"

"Somebody get the air down here. Blast the balls off those goddam laundrymen! Where the hell's the air!"

It was coming.

Five Corsairs swooped down from the leaden skies. The tracers of their .50 caliber guns flashed earthward. Rockets darted from their wings. Bombs described their dreadful arcs. Napalm tanks splashed flame. The ground was shaking and quivering. There was a loud explosion. Marines who had poked their heads above the bank witnessed the gruesome sight of torn and sundered bodies flying through the air. They cheered. The order came:

"Let's go get 'em!"

They rose from the stream bed, bayonets fixed, and charged. Grotesque themselves in their lumpy green parkas, they lumbered through the snow. They hurled their grenades and closed with the bayonet. When it was over, the eighteen Chinese who still lived were taken prisoner.

Then, moving slowly, lungs sobbing for breath, a stich in their sides from the exertion of that charge and fight, they regained the stream bed and slogged south.

The column moved on.

But the ridges to the east were steadily filling up with Chinese. Fresh troops had been rushed down from Manchuria, and General Sung had hurried them south. Since noon the roadbound men had been able to see them moving against the skyline in antlike columns. Corsairs had gone down after them. But they hadn't been able to turn them back. Dispersing, the enemy soldiers plunged into inaccessible ravines and draws. Once the planes had passed, they reappeared, moving closer to The Road. Nor could artillery get down at them with any great effect.

As the day grew darker, the Chinese began to play cozy. They penetrated to within three quarters of a mile of the column. When the flank guards went after them, they withdrew. They were trying to draw the Marines into the hills, away from the column. But they were not successful.

Yet, as dusk of December 6 began to fall, their harrying had held the leading troops to an advance of less than half the distance to Koto. By dusk also, it became apparent that the enemy would strike in force at night.

The column did not halt. It kept moving.

It had grown terribly cold in the cockpit of the little observation plane flying down from Hagaru to the blown water-gate bridge. Lieutenant Colonel Partridge had not suspected that flying in Korea could be so much colder than walking. Now they were flying up and down canyon, passing over the gap from every possible angle, and Partridge shivered beneath his parka, trying to force his mittened fingers to be less clumsy in their note-taking. First glance had shown the accuracy of the December 4 reconnaissance report. There was no room for the big Bailey bridge to be maneuvered around those narrow bends. It would have to be a Treadway. Its sections would comfortably span a gap of about eighteen feet between uphill and downhill abutments. And wooden inserts would be needed to allow the passage of both jeeps and tanks.

Partridge gave the pilot the order to fly to Koto. The tiny craft rose out of the canyon. Partridge looked longingly to the south, across the snow-capped peaks toward Hamhung and safety and, above all, warmth. He shivered, shut the seductive notion out of his mind, and began to plan.

At Koto, he telephoned Hamhung to notify units of his First Engineering Battalion to commence the trial air-dropping of sections with the Air Force. He requested Colonel McGraw to alert the 58th Treadway Bridge Company for a bridge-laying job. He also requested aerial deliveries of precut lumber to Koto, and ordered his Cook Company there to begin scavenging for all available bridging material. He covered the alternatives, for, as he had so intemperately assured his general, he had to get a goddam bridge over that gap.

General Smith arrived in Koto-ri at four o'clock in the afternoon of December 6. He flew down from Hagaru by helicopter. In that thin cold air the craft sank quickly to earth. They dropped the last dozen feet like a falling stone, and Smith received a rude jolt to remind him of the frozen terrain which characterized this last jumping-off point from the high Chosin Reservoir plateau.

Immediately General Smith conferred with Colonel Puller. He found that Koto's defenses were superbly organized. Puller had 2,640 Marines, plus 1,535 Army troops, mostly from the Second Battalion of the Seventh Division's 31st Regiment. There were also 25 British Royal Marines. The perimeter held by Puller's men had not been attacked in force since the night of November 28. The men were in good shape, holding heavily fortified lines.

Puller had also ordered hot food and warming tents prepared for the men fighting down from Hagaru. Koto's 400 vehicles had been kept in readiness for their part in the breakout. The tiny airstrip from which Marine observation planes had been operating was being widened. It would receive heavier craft next day. These would evacuate casualties from a medical station also placed in operation.

Koto-ri was ready.

Chinhung-ni was ready, too, after a brief battle in the afternoon. The Chinese had cut The Road at Sudong, two miles to the south. They had popped up where they were not supposed to be, for all The Road lying below Chinhung was supposed to be free of enemy.

But now the Chinese had a roadblock there, and they had pinned down a platoon of Marine engineers encamped around a hydroelectric power plant. They had occupied the ridges above a village and delivered a plunging fire into the engineer camp. The Marines could not move. Their commander, Lieutenant Thomas Glendinning, radioed north to Lieutenant Colonel Schmuck for help.

Meanwhile the Chinese shot down the American flag which Glendinning had flown from his command post. The lieutenant crawled out and replaced it.

"Let's make sure that it stays there," he told his men.

It did. It remained there during the battle which ensued between Schmuck's relieving force and the entrenched Chinese. It still flew while a Forward Artillery Observer called down a heavy covering fire on the Chinese hilltop.

Only then was it hauled down. And the Engineers came marching out of their camp, carrying their wounded, driving their trucks and tractors.

The last thing out was a bulldozer, its blade held high in jaunty salute.

Then the interdiction of artillery fire fell upon all that area.

It was dark on The Road and it was strangely silent. The Chinese had left off their harassing fire on the column. Quickly Colonel Litzenberg sent out the order to press on with all speed. No matter the meaning of the lull, it was a break. Orders were relayed in the black. Irritated voices sliced through the freezing night air.

"Move out, move out!"

"C'mon, boy—off and on. You ain't never gonna get to Koto on yer ass!"

Shadowy shapes lurched forward. No one cursed, no one beat their gums. It would have been a waste of breath. The advance guard moved ahead, their steps quickening with the returning rhythm of movement. Trucks and jeeps and ambulances rolled forward, picking up speed. But the men in front were near exhaustion. Sometimes laggards waited for a truck to overtake them. They seized hold, grasping tailgate chains, allowing themselves to be dragged, turning and twisting like limp rag dolls.

"Leggo that truck! Get the hell up front where you belong!"

They let go, too tired to protest, almost too cold to care. They let go and fought to retain their balance, or went sprawling in the snow, slowly coming up on all fours, pushing themselves erect and stumbling on to regain their comrades.

Gathering speed, the column pushed on for another mile and a half. It struck another roadblock. A bridge across a small stream had been blown. Heavy fire swept the advance guard. The men deployed and crossed the ice. Behind them a bulldozer set to work building a by-pass. In a half-hour it was done. Cautiously the advance guard moved down The Road. The bulldozer chugged slowly across its own handiwork. A jeep followed. No enemy fire. A half-dozen more vehicles ventured across. Still no fire. More and more followed, and as the leading troops drove farther south, perhaps two score vehicles had passed the roadblock.

The Chinese slammed the door.

They had deliberately allowed the leading elements to pass downroad. Now, with mortars and machine guns and converging grenadiers, they were after the train of vehicles. They came in with sudden violence. They hit hardest against the Seventh's regimental train. Two staff officers were killed. Litzenberg's executive officer, Lieutenant Colonel Frederick Dowsett, was wounded, his jeep driver was killed. Machine-gun bullets raked the deployed vehicles. Men in ambulances cried aloud from new wounds. Chaplain Cornelius Griffin entered one of the ambulances to give a dying Marine the last sacraments. A burst of fire swept the interior. A bullet shattered his jaw. The man beside him fell dead.

Now the Chinese were rushing in to hand-grenade range. Marines under Lieutenant Colonel Harris were deployed around the trucks. They fought savagely, hurling the foe back. A battery of 105 howitzers was frantically trundled to the opposite side of The Road. They fired point-blank, at muzzle blast. The guns shook and roared and spewed orange flame. Companies of charging

Chinese emerged out of the dark only to be bowled over by shells primed to explode the moment they sped from the barrel. Range was now measured in feet, and still the howitzers hammered on. It was a desperate struggle, it would end with more Marines killed, among them Lieutenant Colonel Harris, but it would go against the Chinese.

So would another assault against the vehicles of the division train. Here close to 150 Chinese prisoners would be forced to lie on The Road while the battle was joined with their countrymen. But the attacking Chinese, somehow knowing that there were prisoners in the train, began calling to them in their own tongue. The prisoners called back. They began to move from The Road. The Marines aimed their guns both ways. When the convoy moved on again, the number of prisoners would be down to a score.

Here, too, night hecklers would come to the rescue. They would drop through clouds that had suddenly lifted, finding targets illuminated by the flames of burning trucks. Here headquarters service troops would fight from ditches, musicians of the division band would man machine guns. The enemy would be contained here, too, but at daylight a body of about a hundred Chinese would penetrate to within thirty yards of the convoy. And here would occur perhaps the most dramatic individual fight of the march to Koto-ri.

As the patrol penetrated, the Chinese separated into squads. They attacked with grenades. One squad came at a point held by First Lieutenant Charles Sullivan. Sullivan leaped to his feet. He stood silhouetted by the flames of crackling, roaring trucks, an embattled giant six feet four inches tall, weighing 250 pounds. He emptied his carbine, but he could not stop them all. A half dozen more were closing. The first of them was fifteen feet away. Sullivan bellowed a wordless shout, an atavistic battle cry, and hurled his bayoneted carbine like a javelin. It struck the man in the chest. It transfixed him. His comrades turned and fled.

So the battles were fought while the column punched past the roadblock and swung down The Road into Hell-Fire Valley. Another barrier. Twisted and charred vehicles of Task Force Drysdale had been shoved together in a jumble. Again, the bulldozers growled into action. They battered at them, backing and butting with their powerful noses. They shoved them aside. The column moved on.

"Hello . . ."

It came faintly, from a little hut off to the right. It came again, in a quaint singsong.

"Hello . . . hello, GI . . ."

A black-robed Korean emerged. He beckoned them toward him. A squad of Marines trotted toward the hut, rifles warily at low port. The Korean pointed inside. They entered. They found the last three living men of those wounded whom the Chinese had placed in the hut nine days ago. They found them and they brought them out in stretchers, carrying them tenderly, smiling as they spoke their comradely assurance that the ordeal was over.

But when they saw the blackened, frostbitten flesh the smiles froze on their lips.

It was a quarter of six in the morning of December 7, and they were coming into Koto-ri.

They came in silently this time, these leading troops of the convoy. They had not the strength to form up, to march. They sought only the shelter of the tents, the sudden sustenance of hot coffee—and then sleep. They sank into instant slumber. Four hours later they were marching north again.

It should have defeated them, this order to march back over ground they had wrested from the enemy. They should not have been capable of rising from that heavy sleep. But they were hauled awake, told that they must rescue a battalion of Marine artillery caught in heavy enemy fire, and ordered north again. They went out, knowing full well that they were leaving infinitely fresher men behind them. They went out, unsolaced by the military sagacity that said their knowledge of the terrain, their experience of the enemy, more than offset the weariness of their bodies. For fighting men can never feed on syllogisms. Their only law is the law of averages. Only discipline can master this. And discipline yoked to the love of comrades is beyond defeat.

So they marched back up The Road to relieve the beleaguered gunners.

And then—deliverance.

The artillerymen had fought free. These exhausted men need march no farther. They needed only to set up blocking positions along The Road, to guard the column now winding down, to send patrols out into the hills to that place where H-E-L-P had been stamped in the snow and to rescue those 22 British Marines.

Then they could march back to Koto and go to sleep.

Hagaru-ri was dying. In midmorning of December 7, the little hill town was already alight with its own funeral pyre. Columns of smoke rose everywhere, ascending slowly, thinning, spreading, forming a pall under the overcasts, and beneath this, the fires winked and glowed. Engineers

and demolition men had put everything combustible to
the torch. Huts burned. Bungalows crackled. Oil-soaked
buildings in the railway yard were on fire. Huge piles of
canned rations, soaking for days in heavy oil, now smol-
dered and smoked intermittently.

Up on the ridges around East Hill, Lieutenant Colonel
Roise's battalion was coming down to form the rear guard.
Once descended, the demolitions would begin. But they
began too soon. Hagaru began to rock and erupt. The
hills shook. Fragmenting shells slashed the air. Rockets
blew up. Splinters, steel, boulders, clods of frozen earth
fell in a rain.

Screaming their outrage, pulling their heads down into
their shoulders, Roise's men came hurrying down the hills
out of the impact area. By the time they were down, it
was no longer possible to see Hagaru. It was obscured by
a black cloud, which was sometimes illumined by the flashing of a particularly heavy explosion. When they had
crossed the last bridge out of town, the engineers erased
it with a final, spectacular charge.

Hagaru was dead. Only charred remains had been left
for those Chinese who would be rooting in the rubble within
another quarter-hour.

And already, under cover of the smoke, hundreds of
Koreans were streaming south, crossing the ice on foot
and in bullock carts, hurrying to catch up with the departing Americans.

The news from the south had been bad, and then, won-
derfully good. Lieutenant Colonel Partridge had been
told that the 2,500-pound steel bridge sections had been
hopelessly damaged in trial air drops. But then special
parachutes had been flown to Yonpo from Japan, accom-

panied by a crew of expert Army riggers. They had
worked all night, fitting new sections with the parachutes.
They had loaded them aboard eight Air Force C-119's.
On the morning of December 7, the Flying Boxcars began
taking off.

By half past nine, three of the sections had floated
safely to earth within the Koto-ri perimeter. By noon, the
remaining five had been dropped, though one fell outside
the lines and was lost to the enemy. Two of four wooden
inserts were also recovered. These would be slipped between the metal spans to accommodate the wheeled vehicles.
While the tanks crossed on the metal, the narrower trucks
and jeeps could cross with one wheel on the steel, the
other on the wooden centers.

Quickly material for a complete bridge was loaded on
one Brockway truck. Spare parts went aboard a second.
Slowly, ponderously, these powerful heavy vehicles rolled
downroad to the edge of the southern perimeter. They
halted. They waited, their motors running intermittently
to guard against the cold.

Next morning, with the attack toward Chinhung, they
would roll on again.

The Koreans came out from beneath the smoke. They
came in no ordered procession like the martial column they
sought to overtake. They came in small groups, singly,
in pairs, these civilians. They were the human debris
thrown up by the terrible, incomprehensible war that had
passed their way. They were its most pitiful casualties.
They were hungry, cold, and homeless. Their towns had
been flattened, their mountain huts and villages shattered
or razed. All that bound them now were family ties and
the dread of the Communists they were fleeing—fleeing

them not to escape any wanton savagery, fleeing them because the Chinese were colder and hungrier then they were. The Communists had already taken their young men. Now, in the cruel necessity of warfare, they would need their food, the labor of their limbs. So the Koreans abandoned their towns and villages and fled south.

They had their meager possessions heaped in bullock carts. And many of these were drawn by hand. The beasts had died or had been killed for food. Others carried what they owned in crude bundles strapped to their backs. Here was a twelve-year-old Korean boy plodding ahead in his lumpy black robe with a baby sister or brother swaddled in rags and strapped to his back. Here was a mother stumbling south, prodding her little ones forward, gasping her commands, carrying a bundle of life in her arms. Here were those ancients, the old men of Korea, with their creased and wrinkled faces, these patriarchs of a patriarchal land whose prestige had gone up in a puff of shellfire, whose authority had collapsed as the merely traditional, the merely moral, when matched against the authority of these monster contending powers with heavy artillery to back their wills. They were mocked even by the clothes they wore, the discarded uniforms of the rival armies. Here was a patriarch in American khaki, there was an old man with a parka pulled over a quilted coat. Thus, in their misery, did they seek comfort in the powers that had caused it.

So they overtook the tail of the column driving south. They came from Hagaru and also, now, from the surrounding lowlands. They sought safety in the numbers and the arms of those marchers of the Fifth Marines. But it was no place for civilians. This was a fighting column.

Gunfire still raked it. Refugees were also targets of those
indiscriminate bullets. The Marines could do nothing to
protect them. Though they warned them off, trying to ex-
plain the danger, many still plodded alongside the trucks,
clinging to the treacherous sanctuary of the column.

And then one of the convoys came under enemy fire. A
Korean woman sank to the roadside. There was a child in
her arms. She held it up to a truck driver, choking out the
foreign words of entreaty. The driver didn't see her. All
his faculties were concentrated in holding his big vehicle
to the slippery road, to running the gantlet of fire. But a
big Marine sergeant in the truck saw her. He pulled himself erect on his frostbitten feet and leaned over the side
to take the child. The woman tried to get up but could not.
A corpsman dropped from a truck and ran forward to
aid her.

The big sergeant's truck rolled on. It passed out of gun
range. The sergeant looked at the child. It was a little
boy. His feet were frozen, his tiny uncovered hands
cracked and bleeding. The sergeant propped himself
against the side of the truck. He hunched forward and
huddled the little boy in his arms. He sat still for hours,
sometimes taking a dead pipe from his mouth to croon to
the child when he awoke and cried. It grew dark, and the
truck still ground downroad. There were more outbreaks
of enemy fire. The sergeant remained in the truck. Sometimes the Chinese fired white phosphorous shells, those
searing bursts which terrified both sides in Korea. The
sergeant kept to the truck, sucking on his pipe.

At last it was over. The tail of the column was coming
into Koto-ri. The truck stopped. For the first time in nine
hours the big sergeant moved his body. He swiveled his

feet around and over the end of the truck and hopped painfully to earth. Still clutching the sleeping child, he hobbled through the snow to a medical aid station.

It was after eight o'clock on the night of December 7, and thus, in the experience of a man and a boy, did the last of the Marines come down to Koto-ri.

CHAPTER NINETEEN

IT WAS close to ten o'clock. All of the troops from
Hagaru were now in Koto. Two days of fighting had cost
the First Marine Division 120 dead and missing, 506
wounded. Chinese losses could only be estimated, but
again, they would be enormous. The carnage at East Hill
could be multiplied by relentless scourging from the skies,
those numerous roadblock battles, and the murderous
muzzle-blasting of the artillerymen.

Now, Major General Oliver P. Smith had some 14,000
men to lead south. There were about 12,000 Marines, the
remainder United States soldiers and South Koreans,
about 150 British Royal Marines. Koto's tight perimeter
was dangerously stuffed with humanity. Any sudden onslaught, any abrupt appearance of enemy artillery, un-
foreseen though it might be, could turn it into a slaughter
pen.

General Smith had seen clearly that they had to get
out fast. With daybreak, in fact. He had issued a new
marching order, revising the old one that had guided the
breakout from Hagaru. Litzenberg's Seventh would still
lead the attack, while Murray sent his Fifth against a

hill mass a mile above the water-gate bridge. Puller would
hold Koto with two battalions of his First Regiment and
his battalion of Army.

Puller's other battalion, the First, would be marching
up from Chinhung meanwhile. They had already been relieved there by the Army's Task Force Dog. They would
seize that last barrier, Hill 1081, or The Big Hill, as it
was being called. Then with the bridge rebuilt, The Big
Hill held, The Road would at last be clear for the first
time since November 27.

Puller would then relieve Murray, who would fall in
behind Litzenberg. The regiments would strike south in
that order, Seventh, Fifth, First, down to Chinhung, descending the mountains to the plains of Hamhung, on to
Hungnam on the sea.

That was the plan. It turned on many pivots, but it
swung most of all around the bridge and The Big Hill.

It was ten o'clock, and Smith suddenly became aware
that his chief of staff was shaking his fingers and grimac-
ing with pain.

"What's wrong, Williams?"

"My hands," Colonel Williams replied, gazing at his
fingers in mild astonishment. "Damned if they don't seem
to be frostbitten. They're turning blue."

General Smith was also surprised. There was nothing
wrong with his own hands, and the two men had been
within the heated headquarters tent most of the time.

"How'd that happen?"

"It must have been when I went outside to talk on the
radio jeep. But, hell, I kept sticking my hands in my
pockets, shifting the phone from hand to hand. I was only
out there a few minutes. And look—the damn things are
blue!"

General Smith shrugged. It was a bitter land, well enough. Not even Genghis Khan would have tried it in winter. "Maybe you'd better get some codeine from Hering," he said. "I'm going to turn in soon."

Colonel Williams nodded. He bundled himself up and went out. He was back in a few minutes. He took the pills, and General Smith lay down on a cot to sleep.

But he could not. He was worrying. For the first time since Communist China had entered the war, for the first time since he had found himself with a division of Marines strung out piecemeal along a frozen mountain road without flanks or hope of help, for the first time since then, Oliver Smith began to fret. He lay on his cot and felt his optimism falling from him like a warm cloak. He worried about Partridge and his bridge. He worried about The Big Hill. Did Schmuck have enough men to take it? It was snowing out, which would be good for Schmuck, but bad for Partridge. He worried about these things and a dozen others, feeling at last the leaden weight of despair pressing upon the burden of responsibility he bore.

Then General Smith heard singing.

He propped himself on his cot and listened. It was coming from a nearby tent filled with drivers. General Smith listened, half expecting to hear the voices raised in a depressing bawdy ballad, half hoping for something better —a college song, perhaps, or an old favorite.

And they were singing the "Marines' Hymn."

He heard it, but he could hardly believe that he heard. It was almost too romantic, for Marines rarely sing this song in battle, though men who write propaganda say they do. He listened.

. . . and to keep our honor clean.
We are proud to bear the title
of United States Marines.

The voices were no longer faint, growing in volume as
they swung into the second verse.

Our flag's unfurled to every breeze
From dawn to setting sun.
We have fought in every clime and place
Where we could take a gun—
In the snow of far-off northern lands
And in sunny . . .

General Oliver Smith listened to the end, and then he
lay back on his cot. He felt his optimism flowing back to
him. His men had given it back to him. Here he had lain,
the optimist in battle, the commander who cautioned his
leaders never to betray the slightest hint of pessimism
before the men—and here he had lain in a very mire of
pessimism and it was the men who had lifted him out of it.
It had gone full cycle, this optimism, and now it was back
at its starting point.

He gave himself to sleep. They'd get the bridge, they'd
get the hill, they would get out. And the snow?

Let it come down.

CHAPTER TWENTY

IT CAME down in a fine dry powder. It was a silent, steady snowfall, for the wind no longer wailed and there was not a breadth of air to ruffle it. It laid a hush upon the hills. By three o'clock in the morning of December 8, it lay in a depth of six inches above the perimeter of Chinhung-ni.

Here the men of the First Battalion, First, were gathering for their assault march on The Big Hill a little less than four miles up The Road. They were traveling light. Only two ambulances and a radio jeep would keep to The Road. All other heavy equipment had been sent to the rear by Lieutenant Colonel Schmuck. The Marines were without sleeping bags or rations, carrying only extra ammunition, shoe-pacs, and extra socks which were kept dry against their flesh. For they were going the hard way, overland. Under cover of the snow, concealed by the hills, they counted upon surprise to hurl an outnumbering, well-entrenched enemy from the last barrier between the division and the sea. As snow and a dark river had brought Washington in on the Hessians at Trenton, so snow and dark hills would bring these Americans in on the Chinese in Korea.

Schmuck's battle plan was simple. His reconnaissance a week ago had shown him where the Chinese strength lay. It was concentrated atop and around the crest of The Big Hill, which reared its blunt peak to the right as he faced uproad. Captain Robert Barrow's Able Company would go against this, moving over a narrow hogback. Below Barrow, between the peak and The Road, would be Baker Company, led by Captain Wesley Noren. The Marines of Baker Company would traverse the slopes, descending only to force roadblocks. Their mission was to command The Road. Charlie Company would be in reserve.

At three o'clock they moved out.

It was already 14 degrees below zero. Visibility was almost nil. The men of Able Company were already climbing. Within a few hours they would ascend from 1,200 feet above sea level to an elevation of 3,500 feet. They clutched at rocks or bushes for handholds. They formed human chains to pull one another up the rises. Their hogback was narrow, and beneath the snow the ground was frozen and slippery. Men slipped and fell heavily, the soft new snow hardly cushioning their collision with that iron earth. They had many hours to go before they fought and already there were casualties. Marines with badly turned ankles, with bruised bones and sprains, whimpered softly at the redoubled pain of their progress. But they kept going. For this was Able Company. "Able, Able— hot to go!" That was their cry. They called themselves hard-chargers. They had a good skipper. Captain Barrow had told them that wars were fought by men, had taught them to yell and shout when they closed with the enemy. They had been sheepish about it at first. But they had seen how their rebel yells and battle cries had struck terror among the startled Reds in the streets of Seoul. They had learned to fight the old way, as men on foot with weapons in their hands and shouts on their lips. So they kept moving, toiling over the hills, drawing silently closer to an unsuspecting foe.

Below them, Baker Company slowed its movement to remain abreast. They were finding the slopes too steep and were coming down to roadside. They were hitting roadblocks. But they knocked them out. When they approached these barriers of logs and sandbags, the Chinese fired at them. The Marines drew back, studying the zones of fire. They saw that they were fixed. The enemy could not cover the entire roadblock zone. So the Marines skirted it, bringing up their own machine guns and mortars to hammer the Chinese gun positions.

By ten o'clock in the morning they had burst through three roadblocks. Their guns drove the surprised Chinese from bunkers in the ridges, and Lieutenant Colonel Schmuck was quick to possess one of these as a headquarters. It was a sturdy structure, able to withstand all but heavy artillery fire. It was made of logs, revetted with rice bags filled with sand. Brush had been piled on its sandbagged roof for camouflage, and the snow had given it the aspect of a natural mound of earth. As Captain Noren had guessed, the abandoned guns were rigidly fixed to fire straight down The Road. As he had not known, the Chinese had been eating when he attacked. Schmuck found a bowl of hot rice on a stove. Some of the occupants had been doing their laundry. Garments hung up to dry were still warm. Obviously the Chinese had not been long gone.

Schmuck set up his mortars and settled down to receive reports of the battle.

Outside his bunker the snow had changed. It swirled heavily now, in thick flakes the size of nickels. The wind was rising. It was a blizzard.

It howled wildly about the men of Able Company moving along the hogback. It threw flakes in their eyes. It plastered them with a mantle of white. It covered their approach. Visibility was now less than a hundred yards, as morning turned into afternoon and these Marines closed to within a half mile of the first ridge beneath the summit of The Big Hill. They knew the enemy was out there, for they could hear their voices. But they could not see him. And the enemy at last knew that he was in peril, for he had heard the firing on The Road. But he had no knowledge of the column of martial snowmen plodding toward him through the blizzard. And the wind rose and fell, whipping the snow in slanting sheets, swirling it, shredding it into rifts.

Through one of these rifts Captain Barrow saw the enemy.

They were not two hundred yards away, moving about the crest of that first ridge. The rift filled once more with driving snow and they were lost to sight. They had not seen the Marines.

Barrow's column drew still closer, then halted. The men caught their breath while the skipper attempted to lay mortar fire on the Chinese. But the mortar observers could not calculate targets through that wall of snow. Barrow tried bringing the shells in by sound. The thump and crash of 81mm and 4.2-inch mortar shells rose above the keening of the wind. The ground around the waiting men began to shake. They glanced nervously at each other. Barrow ordered a cease fire. It was too dangerous.

He called his men to the attack. They drove forward.

Atop the ridge the Chinese huddled in their bunkers and peered anxiously into the snow. They, too, had felt the ground shaking, had heard the crash of shells. Were they under attack, or had they been hammered at long-range again as on that dreadful day a week before? They began firing blindly into the storm.

Still, Barrow's men drove forward. They took cover behind rocks, in holes, in crevices, rising to crawl forward whenever the enemy fire slackened. Now Barrow was in position. He sent a squad to either side of the ridge. They would work around it, steal up it, and before dark all but a small reserve of Able Company would charge together.

The Chinese were frantic. Small mortar shells were raining in on them. They *were* under attack. There *were* Americans in the hills, out in that storm. But where?

And the terrible answer came out of the snow.

They burst from the blizzard, these Marines of Able Company, and they fell upon the Chinese with blazing weapons and hurtling grenades. They came on an instant, screaming like devils and bellowing those horrible hoarse cries.

"Yaaaa—hoo!"

"Kill! Kill!"

All of those Chinese who had been above ground were cut down. They had tried to flee. They had scurried wildly about their hilltop, running this way and that, but everywhere they had blundered into those charging, bellowing wraiths. So they had gone down, and only the bunkers held out.

They fought on, and then the Marines were in on them and it was all over.

The ridge had fallen. Out in the storm, beyond and above it, was the towering pinnacle of The Big Hill.

Tomorrow that would fall.

Snow and the enemy were working against the bridge-builders.

At noon of December 8, the big Brockways lumbered down toward the gap. Ahead of them the Marines had begun attacking. But the Chinese clung tenaciously to a system of interlocking bunkers stretching south from the gap all the way up to The Big Hill. The storm protected them from aerial assault, and they fought back viciously with automatic weapons and mortars, especially on high ground to the right of The Road which had been assigned to the battered Third Battalion, Seventh. These riflemen, now led by Major William Morris since the death of Lieutenant Colonel Harris, could make scant progress against the dogged Chinese. Morris reported the situation to Litzenberg. The Seventh's commander radioed back: "Commit your reserve company." And Morris replied: "All three companies are up there—fifty men from George, fifty men from How, thirty men from Item. That's it!"

That was it, 130 men left from an entire battalion, 13 per cent of its original effective force of about 1,000 men, and that was how it went throughout the day. Even after the Second Battalion, Seventh, launched an attack aimed at getting to the enemy's rear, the hill mass still held out. And with darkness closing down, Colonel Litzenberg ordered the bridge trucks to the rear. He would not risk them or their precious cargo to the chance of Chinese shellfire.

The Brockways swung around. They returned to Litzenberg's command post. Here, they were ordered to a safe place to the side of The Road. It appeared to be a cleared parking space. Jeeps and trucks were drawn up on it. The first Brockway, bearing an intact bridge, rolled onto it.

It was a frozen pond.

It gave way.

With the sharp snapping sound of cracking ice, the elephantine vehicle sank up above its radiator in water. Its motor went dead. It was stuck.

And now commenced a most harrowing half-hour for Lieutenant Colonel Partridge and his engineers. They were sick. They stood in the snow, watching through slitted eyes, while the second Brockway was brought up to rescue its brother from the pond. Its powerful motor roared. Its big tires spun in a humming blur of movement, throwing up snow and lumps of earth while it strained to pull the bridge truck free. At last there was a great shout of relief. The drowned truck was being dragged out of the pond. It emerged, an ice-coated mastodon no longer capable of anything but to be towed uphill to Koto-ri. Its motor was useless.

Tomorrow they would try again.

In Koto-ri they were burying the dead. They had hoped to bring these 117 bodies out with them. But some vehicles had to be left open for the inevitable wounded. They had to hold another mass burial.

Snow-covered, blanketed shapes lay in the hollow of an artillery excavation. Above it, two bulldozers stood in readiness alongside humps of excavated earth. The voices of the chaplains rose, intoning:

"Remember, man, that dust thou art . . ." Clods of

frozen dirt fell on the bodies. ". . . unto dust thou shalt
return . . ." The bulldozers roared. ". . . out of dust shalt
thou rise again." The earth of Korea closed over these
Americans.

An artillery aiming stake was driven into the earth as
a marker. Sorrowing onlookers walked slowly back to their
units. For the last time they buried their dead.

But tomorrow there would be more.

All day they had been flowing down The Road from
Hagaru. They had washed up against the Marine roadblock above Koto-ri in a torrent of suffering humanity.
They had been held up there, as against a dam, and now
out before the unhappy Marines stretched a sea of refugees. There were thousands of them. They flooded The
Road, spilling out to either side and eddying in a black
mass up the snow-covered slopes. Some of them tried to
build fires against the cold. But frozen wood is difficult
to burn in wind and driving snow. It is harder to find a
place to burn it when the drifts are four feet deep.

They wanted to get into Koto. They clamored for it.
The murmur of their entreaties rose like a massive lament,
and sometimes the Marines put their fingers into their
ears to shut out the pitiful wailing of these wretched people.

They could not let them in. They could not risk the
Communist strategem of infiltrating in civilian clothes.
They could not hazard the chaos that might ensue should
this flood of people burst inside a perimeter then preparing for a fighting breakout. They could only hold them
there and pray to God that the Chinese would not come
down The Road to begin firing over their heads. Just this,
and give medical aid to those who needed it most. Such

as the two poor women who gave birth to children in the night.

And tomorrow there would be many, many more of them.

In the night the enemy tried to retake Able Company's ridge. They came in a co-ordinated assault. Captain Barrow reported the result to Lieutenant Colonel Schmuck:

"Enemy counterattacked at 0100. We killed them all."

CHAPTER TWENTY-ONE

It was a new day, cold, clear, and bright. The hills were white and gleaming. Sunlight sparkled on the new snow. It beamed on the huddled Korean masses to the north. It cast a welcome light on the engineers working at the water gate. It warmed the wind-blown faces of the men of the column's attacking battalions, closing in once more on the enemy bunkers. It shone clearly on the crest of The Big Hill, though its rays brought only terror to the hearts of its defenders. For they could see the sun glinting off the silvery wings of the American warplanes coming to destroy them.

Corsairs, Hellcats, Mustangs, and attack bombers were already at work in the early morning of December 9. Rocketing, bombing, and strafing, they softened the enemy for the last desperate thrust.

And below The Big Hill the day was greeted by the crackling of gunfire on Able Company's ridge. It alarmed battalion headquarters. An urgent message went out:

"Are you under attack up there?"

"No," Barrow radioed back. "We're just test-firing our weapons."

It was well that they had, for many of them were frozen. The bitterness of a night in the open had already taken its toll. Dozens of men were unable to walk. Before the battle of The Big Hill was over, Schmuck's battalion would suffer 190 casualties from cold alone. Evacuation of the dead and wounded had been an ordeal. Though it had taken a man but an hour and a half to ascend Barrow's ridge, it took evacuation parties five hours to get their burdens down again. It required six men to a stretcher, carrying them in relays, for even six men had not the strength to make the entire trip. For sustenance the men had eaten snow. And now, in this clear but terribly cold morning, having discarded the frozen weapons and replaced them with those taken from casualties, Able Company was hot to go again.

Barrow could see the Chinese on the crest, five hundred yards away. There were many of them, very active, moving quickly about as though preparing their defenses. Barrow's machine gunners and riflemen opened up on them. Even at that range it had telling effect. Chinese began falling. The rest broke for cover. Soon only the sandbagged roofs of the bunkers—about a foot and a half above the ground—were visible from Barrow's ridge.

Able Company attacked.

Under cover of a deafening barrage of supporting arms —large and small mortars, rocket launchers, artillery— they began their ascent. And again they attacked with divided forces, platoons moving around either side of the height, lumbering forward as skirmishers. The Chinese fought valiantly and with skill. Machine guns had been laid in to support the bunkers. These raked the charging Marines. The Chinese battled from cleverly concealed bunkers of which the Marines had no knowledge until they blundered into them. It became a war of hand grenades.

Chinese potato mashers came hissing downhill. The American pineapple grenades went spiraling up. The enemy had more grenades and had gravity on their side. They could throw farther. But the Marines were more accurate and had better grenades. Gradually, inexorably, the figures in the green parkas came higher and higher up the hill. At last they possessed all of the ground surrounding it. They were 150 yards from the crest. They hid behind boulders, took cover in scrubs of wood, and poured a withering fire into the bunkers.

And now Captain Barrow called for air support.

The Marine fighters on station needed little direction from the air control officer. A double telephone pole rose from the middle of the crest, cleaving the air like twin aiming stakes. The warplanes guided on them, snarling down from the clear skies, strafing on the first pass, following through with 265-pound fragmentation bombs and rockets. Eight planes made five passes each. When they had gone, they had blackened the top of the hill, leaving it a dirty smudge against the white purity of the horizon.

The Marines were ready to go again. They stripped enemy bodies of their remaining grenades—for their own had been expended—and tensed for the last attack. Suddenly someone shouted:

"There comes the division!"

They looked below them. They glanced down the steep, glistening slopes of the wicked height they had ascended, and they saw, coming cautiously around a bend, the figures of the leading patrol of the column.

"It's the division!" they yelled. "It's the division! Goddamit, now we *gotta* take that hill!"

"Let's go," roared Staff Sergeant Ernest Umbaugh.

"C'mon, you sons of bitches—let's go get killed on that high ground up there!"

And they went.

They went up to the high ground, where Sergeant Umbaugh himself was killed, charging without cover or supporting arms, fighting bunker by bunker, grenading and being grenaded, until at last not one of those valorous, unflinching defenders was left alive on the crest of The Big Hill. None had chosen to flee, and none had survived. At least 300 enemy dead lay in the bunkers or atop the torn and blackened earth. Several hundred more were scattered about the surrounding ridges.

By half past four in the afternoon, The Big Hill had fallen.

And of the 223 men of Able Company whom Captain Barrow had led against it, 111 of them would come down again.

By noon the Chinese fortifications commanding the water-gate bridge had fallen. They had collapsed under furious aerial assault and been cleaned out by riflemen. One platoon of Marines, crossing the slope behind the gatehouse, had come upon 50 silent Chinese. They were frozen in their holes. The Marines lifted them out, some stretched out straight, others crouched or in sitting positions—like metal dummies in toy vehicles—and carried them down to The Road. They were picked up there and placed on trucks. Some of them would die.

Now with a weapons company deployed across the gap to protect them, the engineers worked to rebuild abutments. Some time after Partridge's reconnaissance, the Chinese had widened the gap to twenty-three feet. And there were Chinese, now—prisoners—laboring to reduce it. The bridge was ready for placement by three o'clock.

The remaining Brockway truck rolled forward, bearing the bridge which had been removed from its ruined twin. It stopped. Gently it began lowering the 2,500-pound sections into place. A half-hour later the gap was spanned.

Elated, Lieutenant Colonel Partridge drove back up the hill to inform the waiting train of vehicles that all was ready. They began rolling down the grade. The leading vehicle approached the Treadway span. And it halted there.

Bad news had come from the south. The advance guard had encountered a serious roadblock. During the night the Chinese had dropped a cable-car trestle down to The Road at a hairpin turn. It would have to be removed, for that tremendous train of 1,400 vehicles could never get by it. Again the engineers went forward. While they struggled to remove this new barrier, the column from Koto-ri was brought steadily forward to the lip of the Treadway. They were bumper to bumper, backed up for miles, patiently awaiting word that The Road was again clear.

The good news came at six o'clock.

Cautiously the first jeep inched onto the Treadway, one wheel on metal, the other on wood. It crossed. There was a weak cheer. Now others. Perhaps a half dozen got over.

Now came the heavy equipment—two snowplows, tractors, big trailers carrying construction gear. The blades of the plows rode up over the angles, lifting the tractor, juggling the sections spanning that yawning gulf. But they got over. Now came a huge bulldozer hauling an eight-cubic-yard earth pan.

Disaster.

The centerboard cracked and collapsed. The big dozer and its earth pan was stuck out in the middle of the bridge, jammed at a precarious angle. Should it fall, it would seal The Road forever. Should it remain there, it would block it just as effectively. The column was again bottled up.

In the darkness an engineering technical sergeant named Wilfred Prosser came forward to volunteer his services. He was known to be an expert driver. He thought he could back the bulldozer safely off the bridge. Partridge gave him his consent. Prosser climbed aboard the tractor. With his rearward path illuminated by flashlights, with the surrounding hills still crackling and rumbling with the noise of battle, and with that dreadful abyss beneath him, he began backing off. The dozer moved gently, almost imperceptibly. Prosser got it off the bridge.

Now the engineers hastened to pull the broken centerboard and the snapped spacer bars off the Treadway. Sheer manpower moved the steel sections. But it was not enough. A tractor blade was skillfully manipulated so as to lift the sections and place them as far apart as possible. Now, a jeep or a truck could move within them. Their tires would grip the sections' inboard lips, they would have a half inch of purchase to spare on either side, they would have nothing but the black air beneath them, but they could get across. Tanks and other tracked vehicles would have two inches to spare on either side. And they, too, would get across.

An hour later the column started forward. While Chaplain John Craven guided the drivers by flashlight, the dark bulky shapes rolled up to the gap, positioned their tires for that precarious purchase, and drove onto the other side.

The first of the two barriers had been passed.

Below Funchilin Pass, in the lengthening shadows of The Big Hill, the Marines of Baker Company had destroyed the last and biggest of the roadblocks. They set up positions. Enemy groups came toward their guns, driven downroad by the steady pressure of the column's advancing spearheads. They were raked. They struck off to the east beneath Barrow's guns on The Big Hill. They were riddled. Throughout the night and into the dawn of December 10, this terrible cat's play continued until at last the demoralized remnants drifted farther east into the snow-choked hills.

The last barrier had fallen, and The Road to the sea was now open.

CHAPTER TWENTY-TWO

IT WAS December 10 and they were coming down The Road to Chinhung-ni.

They were moving through Funchilin Pass, debouching into the low ground that let them down the mountainsides. They could be seen by the exulting Marines atop The Big Hill—these lines of marching men, that long dark column of vehicles extending backward for eleven miles.

They were coming down, and there were refugees with them now, for the dam above Koto had at last burst. There were cattle with them, too, and occasionally the crying of a baby rose above the crunching of shod feet on snow, the murmuring of many motors. They were coming down, bringing out their wounded, their dead, their prisoners. There was fighting still going on behind them, below Koto, and they would lose some tanks in the confusion of it, but they were coming down with nearly all of their vehicles and their guns. There would be sporadic skirmishes to the flanks, even a battle below Chinhung-ni, but most of them would survive it—and here they were, coming down that bitter road, descending the glittering cruel hills of northern Korea.

They were coming down, these men of the First Marine Division and the soldiers who marched with them, and they had fought the greatest battle of American arms. They had suffered 7,500 casualties, and with their air had inflicted an estimated 37,500 on the enemy. They had ruined an entire Chinese army group, ten to twelve divisions against their one. So far from having been annihilated by General Sung, they had crippled his command. His Ninth Army Group not only was powerless to push Tenth Corps into the sea, it could not come to the aid of other forces battering the Eighth Army in the west. Hungnam would be evacuated without hindrance, thanks to these marching men who were coming down, thanks to the white-haired general who flew over them in his helicopter, bound for Hamhung, coming down, too, after having conducted perhaps the most perfect division operation in military history.

They were coming down to further battles below the 38th Parallel, for they could guess that they had seen the start of a brand-new war. But they were coming down to this flamboyantly, their scathing scorn for this brand-new enemy emblazoned in red paint on the side of that jaunty tank, at last removed to the tail of the column. It said: "ONLY 14 MORE SHOOTING DAYS UNTIL XMAS." And they were coming down to glory—to Medals of Honor for Private Cafferata and Sergeant Kennemore, for Captain Barber and Captain Sitter, Major Myers and Lieutenant Colonel Davis; posthumous ones for Private Baugh, Sergeant Johnson, and Sergeant Windrich—coming down to the lesser glory of Navy Crosses by the dozen, to hundreds of Bronze and Silver Stars, and to the everlasting glory of their march.

They were coming down to Chinhung, and now this

thing that lifted them, this exaltation, was bursting into song.

They came down singing. Not that "Marines' Hymn" which had given their general back his confidence, for that was a rallying song which they no longer needed. Not a hymn of praise to God, a "Glory, Alleluia" such as had burst from the throats of their forebears, for American warriors no longer sing their faith. Not even a bawdy, for this was now beneath them. They sang a song of derision. It was a sardonic song, one that mocked themselves and bawled out their contempt for the whole wide world. They had been there and back, had been through a hell that blazed and froze by turns, and they were singing their splendid disdain for all those pallid paltry souls who did not go. Their voices rose, bellowing out their own version of the Australian marching song, "Bless 'Em All":

Bless 'em all, Bless 'em all,
The Commies, the U.N. and all.
Them slant-eyed Chink soldiers hit Hagaru-ri
And now know the meaning of "U.S.M.C."
So, we're saying good-by to them all
As home through the mountains we crawl.
The snow is ass-deep to a man in a jeep
But who's got a jeep?
Bless 'em all!

Bless 'em all, Bless 'em all,
The long and the short and the tall.
We landed at Inchon and old Wolmi-do
Crossed the Han River and took Yongdong-po.
But we're saying good-by to it all,
To Hamhung and Hungnam and Seoul.

There'll be no gum-beatin', we're glad
          we're retreatin'
So cheer up me lads
Bless 'em all!

Bless 'em all, Bless 'em all,
The adm'rals an' commodores all.
Bless General MacArthur and bless Harry, too
Bless the whole brass-hatted Tokyo crew.
For we're saying good-by to it all
We're Truman's "police force" on call.
So put back your pack on, the next stop
          is Saigon
An' cheer up me lads
Bless 'em all!

They came down to their great glory singing, their
voices ringing out over the ice like deep-throated bells,
drifting on the wind to the holes and huts which sheltered
the wretched remnants of the enemy.

And when the Chinese heard that singing, they knew
that they had failed.

ABOUT THE AUTHOR

Robert Leckie was a machine gunner and then a scout with the First Marine Division during World War II. His first book, an autobiographical narrative of his experiences with the Marines, was *Helmet For My Pillow* which received the Marine Corps Combat Correspondents Annual Award for 1957. He has also written *Lord, What a Family*, a humorous study of one American family's life in the early 1930's, and *Marines*, a collection of short stories published in 1960.

The author of numerous biographical and critical articles published in national magazines, Mr. Leckie has been active in newspaper work since the age of sixteen. His first job was sportswriter for a New Jersey daily, and since then he has worked for eight newspapers as well as the Associated Press. He has also written documentary films and been the editor of the Telenews Weekly as well as MGM's News Of The Day.

THIS BOOK WAS SET IN

SCOTCH TYPE, PRINTED, AND BOUND

BY THE HADDON CRAFTSMEN.

IT WAS DESIGNED BY ANDOR BRAUN.